ANIMAL
PEOPLE

I0110269

Copyright ©2018 by Joel Goldstein.

ISBN-13: 9780692153031
ISBN-10: 0692153039

Library of Congress Control Number: 2018909096

All rights reserved. No parts of this publication may be reproduced or transmitted in any form or by any means, electronic or mechanical, including photocopy or any other information storage or retrieval system, without prior permission in writing from the author.

The images in this book were collected by Joel Goldstein. Every effort has been made to locate the artist for each image.

This book is dedicated to the booksellers, ephemera dealers, and flea market sellers who preserved and sold the images that made *Animal People* possible.

CONTENTS

JOCKO

Foreword

A late nineteenth century American store display advertising Grove's Tasteless Chill Tonic portrays a pig with a human child's head. The head, secured to a pig's body through the artistic device of a lace collar, is not the only strikingly odd thing about this early advertisement. Written across the pig's midsection are the words "makes children and adults as fat as pigs". As strange as this ad seems to our twenty-first century eyes, it was no less eye-catching to intended nineteenth-century viewers.

This book is a collection of animal-people illustrations which are the antithesis of Grove's Chill Tonic store display. For the most part, this book's animal-people combinations are seamless and strangely attractive, the work of artists well aware of both human and animal anatomy, as well as folk tales and mythology.

The history of animal-people is as old as art itself. A wooden sculpture found in what is now Germany and given the name "lion-man" is estimated to be from between 43,000 to 33,000 B.C. Various versions of animal-people imagery play a large role in the religions and mythologies of ancient cultures, including those of Egypt, Babylon, Greece, India, and Rome. They also appear as tribal, folkloric, and satirical beings throughout Eastern and Western cultural history.

Animal-people had a last burst of popularity in nineteenth-century advertising. Visual advertising relies on eye-catching imagery and the world of animal-people is an assured eye-catching world, a world populated by conundrums.

The late nineteenth-century popularity of the trade card, an advertising giveaway, along with Book illustrations, cigarette cards, and die cut scraps, make up the majority of this book's illustrations. Postcards, which became popular in the early twentieth-century, complete this animal-people menagerie.

Many of the artists who created the more than 400 images in this book are uncredited. In many cases they were employees of printing firms and rarely allowed to sign their work. This book is a tribute to all these skilled and imaginative artists who brought these magical creations into the world.

Introduction

In 1980, while I was working on illustrations for the New York Times Book Review, Steven Heller, the Book Review art director, asked me if I would be interested in working with him on a book proposal. The subject was a history of animals depicted as people throughout the history of visual arts. I believe he asked me both because I was an artist and because I had just finished working as a picture researcher on the book *Air Powered: The Art of the Airbrush* (Random House, 1979).

After agreeing to do the research and prepare a book dummy, I quickly realized that the depiction of hybrid animal-human forms had a history almost as old as visual arts itself. I also came to realize that, even though animal-people existed over the entire history of art creation, this group of unique images remained disdained curiosities of the arts, rarely taken seriously or written about.

What I found most impressive after studying animal-people images over a wide span of both time and cultures was that whether following guidelines through religion, myth, or fable or inventing on their own, these often unknown artists crafted composite beings not just nonexistent in nature but truly works of pure art, both haunting and strangely familiar. The idea failed to find a publisher, perhaps because of the magnitude of the subject; however, some of our research appeared in the form of an article in Print magazine, March–April 1981.

Although work on the book project had ended, my interest in the subject had grown with the material I had uncovered, and I was curious to find out more. Over the following years, I put together a collection of mainly nineteenth-century examples and a library of books relating to the subject and associated topics, including the history of specific animals, folk and mythical narratives, histories of farm and zoo animals, and studies of caricature and satire. These were supplemented by books on printing and graphic and fine arts.

What my research revealed most emphatically was that the nineteenth-century was the century of animal-people throughout both Europe and the United States, but the roots of nineteenth-century fascination with the subject could be traced back to two Frenchmen, one who humanized animals in prose, the other who compared animals with humans through images.

Jean de la Fontaine (1621–1695) was born in the Champagne region of France. For nearly twenty years, he held the office of inspector of forests and waterways, an occupation that put him in close proximity with France's animal population. During these years, he also pursued a career as a poet, reading extensively the works of classical writers as well as French sixteenth- and seventeenth-century authors.

In 1688, he published the first of what would become twelve books containing over two hundred fables. Originally influenced by the fables of Aesop and Phaedrus, la Fontaine's modernized satires of human nature featured a cast of talking animals and combined a profound understanding of human foibles with a poetic lightness and humor. Originally intended for a learned audience, they became a popular success, remaining in print for over three hundred years after their first publication. Their longevity is a tribute to la Fontaine's ability to evoke an imaginary Adamic time when animals shared human concerns and could speak.

La Fontaine was a protégé of Nicolas Fouquet, Louis XIV's minister of finance. Charles le Brun (1619–1690) had worked for Fouquet before being put in charge of the decoration of Versailles as Louis XIV's painter-in-chief. He was also director of the Gobelins factory that produced the furnishings and grand tapestries for the palace at Versailles.

Le Brun's important contributions to the history of animal-people were not enormous murals and furnishings, but two groups of drawings.

The first group of drawings, presented at a meeting of the Academie de Peinture in 1678, was influenced by the sixteenth-century artist Giambattista della Porta's book De Humana Physiognomia. The forty-one animal and human comparisons that le Brun produced range from a Zeus-like mythical head shown above lions sporting similar looks and manes, to five bird heads surrounding two birdlike men. The intent of these drawings was to show that similar physiology can contain faculties and characters in both man and animal.

In 1806, many of these drawings were reproduced to accompany the writings of John Caspar Lavatar. Lavatar, a Swiss pastor, was the popularizer of the pseudoscience of physiognomy, which stressed correspondences between physical appearance and moral character. His writings had a strong influence in France, England, and America, especially on the works of writers and artists.

The second group of drawings, produced in le Brun's capacity as founder, director, and principal theorist of the French Academy, was reproduced as engravings in book form in 1698 and titled Conference sur l'Expression General et Particuliere. The book, a manual for artists (also used by actors and orators), was an attempt to codify, in words and pictures, the principal human passions and their manifestations in facial expressions. Proving highly popular, this book, like la Fontaine's fables, was still being studied and used in the first half of the nineteenth-century.

La Fontaine and le Brun, each in his own manner, had explored the animal-human hybrid, but it wouldn't be until 1829 and the publication of an album of seventy-three lithographs in Paris that animal-people would become a common part of European and American popular culture.

Titled *Les Metamorphoses du Jour*, it created a satirical world, masterfully combining animal and human characteristics. Anatomically correct animals with wonderfully expressive faces were fitted out with human lower bodies and clothed in the garb of tradesmen and bourgeoisie of 1820s France. These animal-people discuss, work, and play out the roles of like-minded humans. But unlike illustrations of a similar satirical genre, which were often meant as a sharp, rapier thrust against a political opponent or pernicious law, these drawings create a complete fantasy world that puts in question a wide range of human customs and passions.

Les Metamorphoses du Jour bore the name "I. Adolphe Grandville" on its title page, but by his next publication, titled Galerie Mythologique, Jean-Ignace-Isidore Gerard (his real name) had adopted the nom de plume "J. J. Grandville."

Grandville, born in Nancy in 1803 into a family connected to the arts and theater, first became popular as an illustrator for the French satirical journals La Silhouette and La Caricature. Although he did produce animal-human images for these publications, it was his book and album illustrations, both on his own and for various authors (including la Fontaine), that were his most brilliant work. From 1829 till his death in 1847, Grandville created thousands of drawings, a large number of which contained his distinct animal-human hybrids. Grandville would become the uncontested master of animal-human imagery, the artist that others would strive to emulate. But few could surpass his uncanny ability to meld human and animal seamlessly and ground them both in a real and surreal world. Works by Grandville were included in the first museum exhibition devoted to surrealism, *Fantastic Art Dada Surrealism*, held at New York's Museum of Modern Art in 1936.

A number of factors allowed these former esoteric images to become so popular in the nineteenth-century. First and foremost was that the majority of people during this time lived in close proximity to a wide variety of domesticated animals, which they relied upon for transport, companionship, sport, recycling, and entertainment. The caring for sick animals and slaughtering of animals for food had not been completely isolated from other household tasks and given over to specialists. Simply put, nineteenth-century Europeans and Americans, whether living in the country or the city, saw, heard, and smelled a large variety of animals in the course of their daily lives.

Charles Dickens, writing in the 1840s about a trip to America, describes a carriage ride down Manhattan's Broadway, where "two portly sows are trotting up behind the carriage and a select party of half a dozen gentleman hogs have just now turned the corner," while in Dickens's own London at about the same time, the famous

Smithfield Market saw the transport of sheep, cattle, pigs, and calves through the city streets depositing approximately 40,000 tons of manure on their journey to the slaughterhouse.

Earlier eras had similar, if less hectic, relations to the animal world, but what made animal-people images significantly more common were innovations in printing and publishing, especially the discovery of stone lithography by the German Aloys Senefelder in 1776. Lithography, which grew in popularity during the nineteenth-century, was a cheaper and speedier way of reproducing illustrations than the labor-intensive wood engraving. This in turn led to rapid growth in both publishing and advertising as the century progressed.

Satirical journals and magazines became the most frequent users of animal-people images. These journals were the province of a small group of readers at the century's beginning but became commonplace in many households by its close.

Advertisers, always ready to adopt any eye-catching imagery, used animal-people images in magazines, trade cards, and posters. The hybrid animal images seem surreal to our eyes now, but it's conceivable that to their original viewers they were both strange and familiar, even comforting in some way, as compared to the strikingly new images of industrial machinery.

Many of the artists working for the satirical journals were influenced by illustrations in physiognomist Johan Caspar Lavatar's books. Though the illustrations in Lavatar's books were meant to stress "scientific" correspondences between physical appearance and moral character, in the hands of these gifted artists the illustrations served as a perfect springboard for biting satire, merging characteristics of human and animal to produce a very different vision.

These same satirical journals had a field day after the publication of Charles Darwin's *On the Origin of Species by Means of Natural Selection* in 1859. For caricaturists and illustrators, the marriage of man and ape, gleaned from Darwin's theories, was heaven-sent, producing a steady stream of humorous drawings during the late 1860s and 1870s and spilling over into the generalized use of animal-people images throughout the graphic arts.

But if these conjunctions weren't enough in highlighting animal and human relationships, the Western world's fascination with both the public zoo and the circus in the nineteenth-century went a long way to integrate exotic and rarely seen animals into the general psyche. Much of this interest in exotic animals grew out of the openings of municipal zoos. The primary zoologic garden, which no doubt fascinated both artists and the general public, was the menagerie at the Jardin des Plantes, founded in Paris in 1793. (Grandville illustrated "A Letter from the Giraffe of the Jardin des Plantes.") This botanical garden, which also housed a selection of mammals, became a template for zoologic gardens worldwide, including the Gardens of the Zoological Society of London, founded in 1828. Many of the zoos, caricaturing Darwin's theories, held shows of clothed, trained monkeys, a practice still in existence at the Saint Louis Zoo's chimpanzee show as late as the 1950s.

The circus, an institution that blossomed in the nineteenth-century, was the other popularizer of exotic animals, acquainting much of the public with their first close viewing of animals previously seen only in books often filled with inaccurate pictures. An 1842 showbill for the American traveling circus of June, Titus, and Angevine headlined the group's show with the claim of "a beautiful Collection of Living Wild Animals comprising the stupendous Giraffe!, the only one now living on the American Continent."

By the early twentieth-century, interest in animals, both real and imagined, had begun to wane. People's daily lives, especially for city dwellers, rarely encompassed chancing by a pig or a goat on their way to work. A letter written in 1909 by the children's book author Beatrix Potter notes the nineteenth century's fascination with clothed animals. Potter, writing about a cat depicted in her book *Ginger and Pickles*, mentions that the cats unusual color is ill served by having to cover him up with coat and trousers.

Ironically, less than ten years after Potter's letter was written, and hastened by the realities of the First World War, the dressed animal became a rarely depicted image outside of children's books and political cartoons and, eventually, a rarity even in those areas as the twentieth century progressed.

In this book, I've concentrated on images from the nineteenth-century and the beginning of the twentieth that depict not just clothed animals but those assuming the postures and facial expressions of humans. I've chosen to limit the use of political caricature, a large body of animal-human images, because such images often favored the joining of a human head to an animal form usually as a way of making a less-than-subtle commentary on a politician or statesman, not truly marrying the two components. I've also steered clear of most children's book examples with the exception of those that retained a realistic or even edgy quality.

This survey of work by artists covering nearly seventy-five years varies in scope, from the master of the genre, Grandville, to many unknown and forgotten artists employed by advertisers, publishers, and postcard manufacturers. Although some of their creations vary drastically in their merging of the animal and human form, they all share in common a mix of animal lore and human foibles contained in a purely invented being—the meeting of related but distant species in the biological world.

A wonderful variety of styles forms the artists' interpretations of each animal, a variety partly dependent on the artists' ability to "humanize" each animal and on their skill to form creations with emotions and facial expressions not found in the animal world but with emotions that the artists had actually felt themselves.

Lionel Lambourne, in his book on Ernest Griset, a nineteenth-century artist who did both realist and animal-people drawings and paintings, aptly sums up the preoccupation by the Victorians with the interrelationship of man and animal as "…part of the recurrent mystery of the anthropomorphic impulse, by which man, by his artistry, achieves the status of God, and remakes creation to his own image."

The proliferation of animal-people images throughout the nineteenth-century was in direct proportion to the loss of animal diversity in daily life. What was once familiar became the stuff of fantasy through art.

APES <small>AND</small> MONKEYS

For his entertainment a King of Egypt had his dancing masters teach some apes the Pyrrhic Dance. The apes dressed in costumes performed for a grand audience.

They danced beautifully until a spectator sprinkled a handful of nuts around them. They then stopped dancing, ripped off their costumes and grappled for the nuts.

Babrius
2nd Century(?)

The Simiadae then branched off into two great stems, the New World and Old World monkeys; and from the latter at a remote period, Man, the wonder and the glory of the universe, proceeded.

The Origin of the Species, Charles Darwin

XLII.

Pour qui sont ces serpents qui sifflent sur ma tête?

ARTIST: J.J. Grandville
Book illustration
1869?, France
Hand colored engraving

ARTIST: Charles H. Bennett
Book illustration
1857?, England
Hand colored lithograph

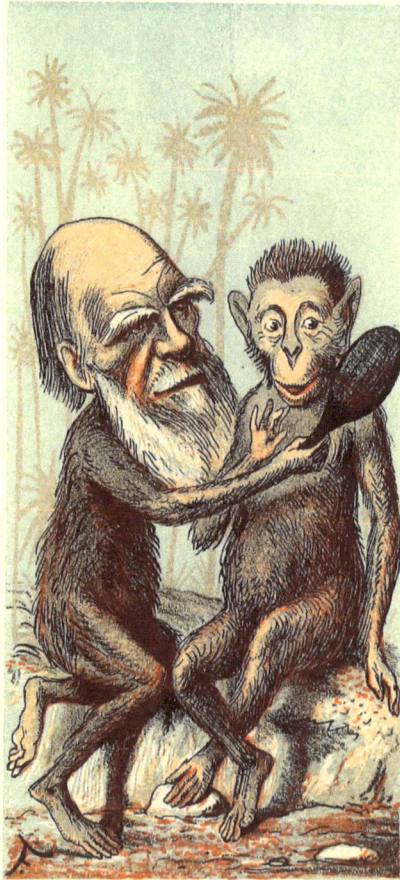

THE LONDON SKETCH BOOK.

PROF. DARWIN.

This is the ape of form.
Love's Labor Lost, act 5, scene 2.

Some four or five descents since.
All's Well that Ends Well, act 3, sc 7.

ARTIST: Unknown
Advertisement
1874, England
Chromo lithograph

ARTIST: Unknown
Trade card
1880's, U.S.A.
Chromo lithograph

MY VALENTINE
PHIL. J. GERHARDY'S
GREAT
SAN FRANCISCO MARKET
Packing and Provision Establishment,
829 & 831 Broadway, OAKLAND, CAL.

This Market has its own Slaughter House, and will sell
Meat 30 per cent. lower than any Market in
Alameda County.

ARTIST: Unknown
Trade card
1880's, U.S.A.
Lithograph

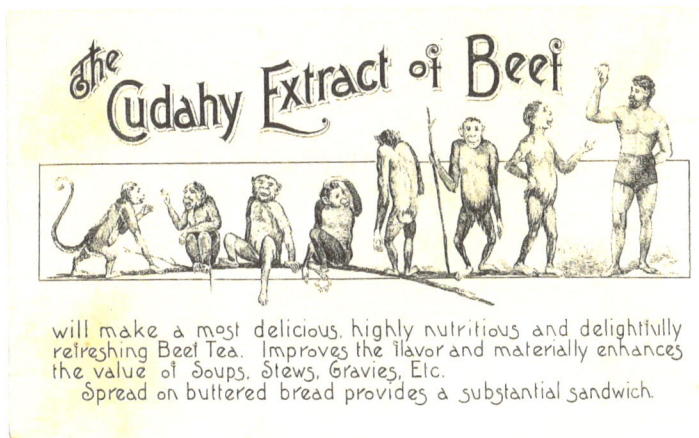

The Cudahy Extract of Beef

will make a most delicious, highly nutritious and delightfully
refreshing Beef Tea. Improves the flavor and materially enhances
the value of Soups, Stews, Gravies, Etc.
Spread on buttered bread provides a substantial sandwich.

ARTIST: Unknown
Trade card
1888, U.S.A.
Lithograph

ARTIST: Unknown
Book illustration
19th C.
Lithograph

ARTIST: Unknown
Stock printer's card
19th C.
Chromo lithograph

Your peer in style, and I suspect.
Your equal, too, in intellect.

ARTIST: Unknown
Penny dreadful
Late 19th C., England
Chromo lithograph

Trying to mash, are you!

ARTIST: Unknown
Trade card
Late 19th C., England
Chromo lithograph

ARTIST: Unknown
Die cut scrap
Late 19th C., England
Chromo lithograph

ARTIST: Unknown
Trade card
1882, U.S.A.
Chromo lithograph

ARTIST: Unknown
Trade card
Late 19th C., England
Chromo lithograph

ARTIST: Unknown
Trade card
Late 19th C., U.S.A.
Chromo lithograph

LUNCHEON BEEF.
· READY · FOR · TABLE · USE ·

Qu'allons nous faire aujourd'hui?

ARTIST: Unknown
Trade card
Late 19th C., France
Chromo lithograph

ARTIST: Unknown
Die cut scrap
Late 19th C.
Chromo lithograph

You Dirty Boy.

BY PERMISSION OF THE PROPRIETORS OF PEARS SOAP.

ARTIST: Unknown
Die cut scrap
Late 19th C.
Chromo lithograph

ARTIST: Unknown
Trade card
1881, U.S.A.
Chromo lithograph

ARTIST: Unknown
Trade card
Late 19th C., U.S.A.
Chromo lithograph

ARTIST: Unknown
Trade card
1881, U.S.A.
Chromo lithograph

BROOKE'S SOAP.

MONKEY BRAND.

For Scrubbing Floors
and Kitchen Tables.

For Metals, Marble, Paint & Glass.

For Steel, Iron, Copper, Bronze.

For Stair-Rods and Mantels.

For a Thousand Household Uses.

The other Side Please!

Won't Wash Clothes!

ARTIST: Unknown
Die cut Trade cards
Late 19th C., England
Lithograph

ARTIST: Unknown
Trade card
Late 19th C., England
Chromo lithograph

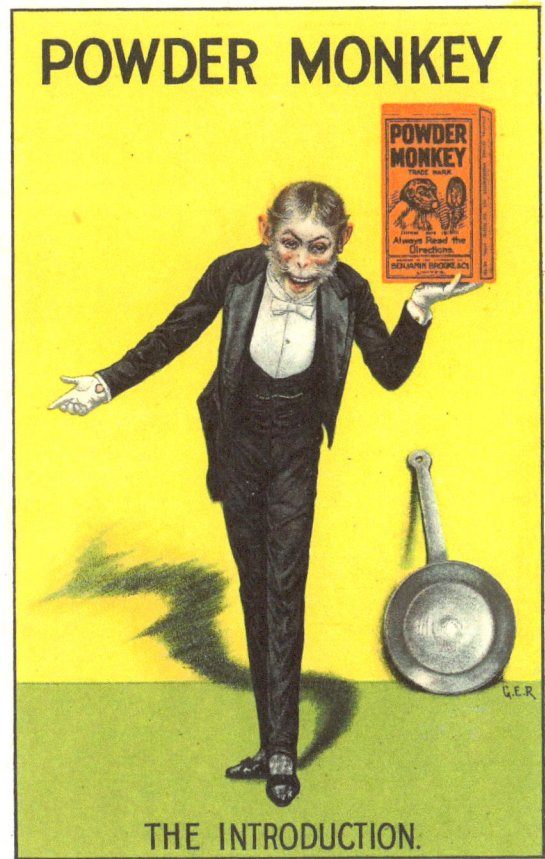

ARTIST: Unknown
Trade card
Early 20th C., England
Offset

ARTIST: Unknown
Advertisement
1901, England
Offset

"BORAXINE"
· MAKES EVERYBODY HAPPY ·

ARTIST: Unknown
Trade card
1882, U.S.A.
Chromo lithograph

"BORAXINE"
SOFTENS THE HARDEST WATER.

ARTIST: Unknown
Trade card
1882, U.S.A.
Chromo lithograph

ARTIST: Unknown
Die cut scrap
Late 19th C.
Chromo lithograph

ARTIST: Unknown
Trade card
1882, U.S.A.
Chromo lithograph

ARTIST: Unknown
Trade card
1882, U.S.A.
Chromo lithograph

ARTIST: Unknown
Die cut scrap
Late 19th C.
Chromo lithograph

"CREME"
OAT MEAL TOILET SOAP

ARTIST: Unknown
Trade card
1882, U.S.A.
Chromo lithograph

"ELITE" TOILET SOAP.
EVERY 25C. BOX CONTAINS A FINE HANDKERCHIEF.

ARTIST: Unknown
Trade card
1882, U.S.A.
Chromo lithograph

ARTIST: Unknown
Die cut scrap
Late 19th C.
Chromo lithograph

JOCKO

ARTIST: Unknown
Die cut scrap
Late 19th C.
Chromo lithograph

ARTIST: Unknown
Die cut scrap
Late 19th C.
Chromo lithograph

ARTIST: Unknown
Paper toy
Late 19th C., U.S.A..
Chromo lithograph

EVERYBODY WHO USES
GLIDDEN'S SHELLAC OIL FINISH
—AND—
GLIDDEN'S NORTH COAST RUBBING
IS HAPPY.

IT IS MADE ONLY BY
THE GLIDDEN & JOY VARNISH CO.
CLEVELAND, OHIO, U. S. A.
BRANCHES: BOSTON—10 CENTRAL ST.,
CHICAGO—278 F. MADISON ST.,
KANSAS CITY—19TH & GENESEE STS.

ARTIST: Unknown
Trade card
Late 19th C., U.S.A.
Chromo lithograph

"ENTERPRISE" ROASTED COFFEE

AN "APE."

ARTIST: Unknown
Trade card
Late 19th C. U.S.A.
Chromo lithograph

J&P.COATS
BEST SIX CORD

ARTIST: Unknown
Trade card
Late 19th C., U.S.A.
Chromo lithograph

Haddock's Cards.

THE 'TOXICATED MONKEY---4 DESIGNS.

The Promenade.--Morning.

COPYRIGHTED BY JNO. A. HADDOCK, PHILA.

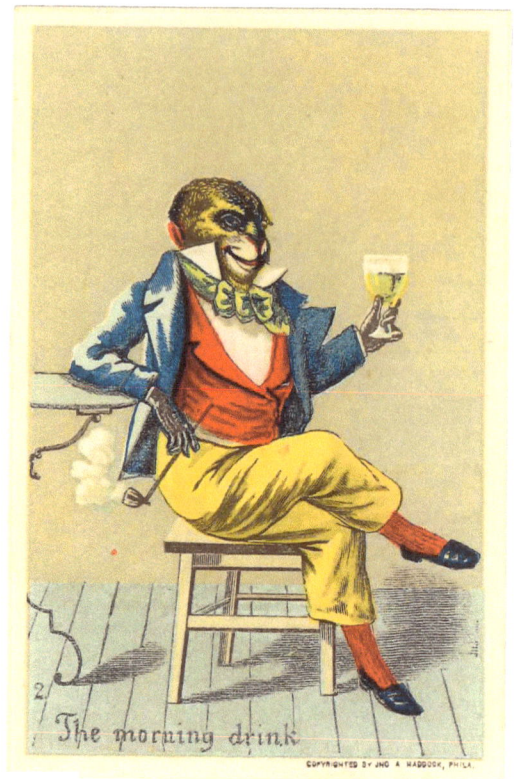

The morning drink

COPYRIGHTED BY JNO. A. HADDOCK, PHILA.

ARTIST: Unknown
Four trade cards
Late 19th C., U.S.A.
Chromo lithograph

ARTIST: Unknown
Die cut scrap
Late 19th C., U.S.A.
Chromo lithograph

3.
Will you dance with me?

COPYRIGHTED BY JNO. A. HADDOCK

Haddock's Cards.
The 'Toxical Monkey.
4 DESIGNS

4.
On his way home ≈ Night.

COPYRIGHTED BY JNO. A. HADDOCK, PHILA.

ARTIST: Unknown
Die cut scrap
Late 19th C.
Chromo lithograph

ARTIST: Unknown
Four die cut scraps
Late 19th C.
Chromo lithograph

ARTIST: Unknown
Trade card
1888, U.S.A.
Chromo lithograph

ARTIST: Tobin
Trade card
Late 19th C., U.S.A.
Lithograph

Wait till the
clouds roll by

122
A

DETROIT MUSIC CO.,
184 & 186 WOODWARD AVE.

PLEIS
Celebrated Fit Powders and Liver Pills,
No. 860 North Third Street,
Philadelphia, Pa.

ARTIST: Unknown
Trade card
Late 19th C., U.S.A.
Chromo lithograph

39

ARTIST: Unknown
Greeting card
Late 19th C., Germany
Chromo lithograph

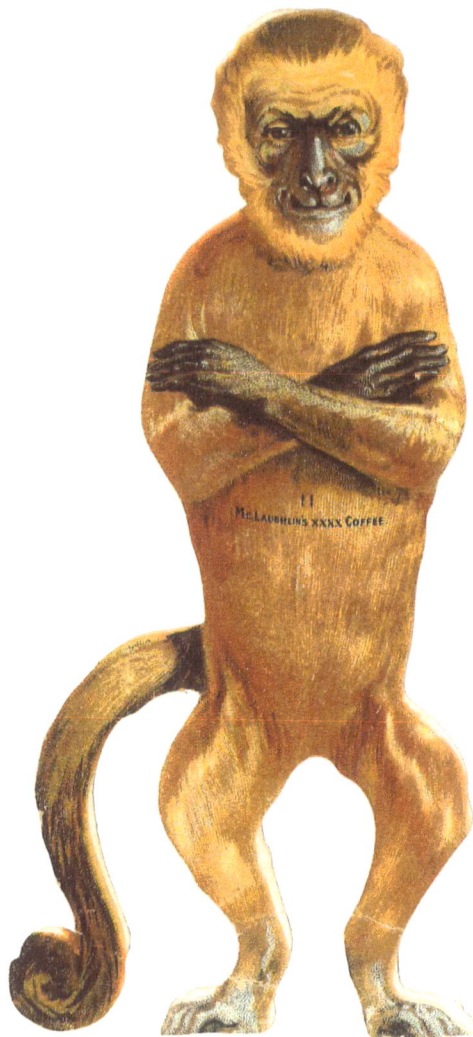

ARTIST: Unknown
Die cut Trade card
Late 19th C., U.S.A.
Chromo lithograph

ARTIST: Unknown
Die cut scraps
Late 19th C.
Chromo lithograph

ARTIST: Unknown
Die cut Trade card
Late 19th C., U.S.A.
Chromo lithograph

ARTIST: Unknown
Die cut Trade card
Late 19th C., U.S.A.
Chromo lithograph

ARTIST: F.R.
Book illustration
1892, U.S.A.
Engraving

ARTIST: Harrison Weir
Book illustration
1892, U.S.A.
Engraving

ARTIST: Unknown
Postcard
Early 20th C., Germany
Lithograph

ARTIST: Unknown
Advertising postcard
Early 20th C., U.S.A.
Lithograph

ARTIST: Unknown
Postcard
Early 20th C., France
Lithograph

ARTIST: Unknown
Postcard
Early 20th C., France
Lithograph

Iedereen wil een bubikop.

ARTIST: H.T.
Postcard
Early 20th C., Dutch
Offset lithograph

ARTIST: Unknown
Postcard
Late 19 C., Germany
Chromo lithograph

ARTIST: Unknown.
Postcard
Late 19 C., U.S.A.
Chromo lithograph

ARTIST: Unknown.
Postcard
Late 19 C., France
Die-cut chromo lithograph

ARTIST: Unknown.
Postcard
Early 20th C., England
Offset

t'en as une tête de singe

ARTIST: V.R.
Postcard
Early 20th C., France
Lithograph

Du stammst von einem
Sagt jeder blanke Spiegel dir!

ARTIST: Unknown.
Postcard
Early 20th C., Germany
Lithograph

L'Incroyable.

ARTIST: Unknown.
Postcard
Early 20th C., France
Offset

BIRDS

"I never start to sing until my eight claws, after clearing a space of weeds and stones, have found the soft, dark turf underneath. Then, placed in direct contact with the good earth, I sing!"

Chantecler, Edmond Rostand

LI.

Vo régardez Milédy

ARTIST: J.J. Grandville
Book illustrations
1829, France
Hand colored engravings

XXXIII.

Un mariage suivant les lois.

A GREEN GOOSE

ARTIST: Unknown
Illustration
Late 19th C.,
Lithograph

And when Bill started to fly away,
Flash! bang! went the gun, making a wound
Which caused poor Bill to fall to the ground!
He dropped into a bush which hid him quite well,
And the farmer, not knowing just where he fell,
Went away, and Bill, when once more alone,
Determined to try and get to his home;

Wicked, naughty, dying Bill.

ARTIST: Unknown
Book illustration
1870's, U.S.A.
Hand colored engravings

ARTIST: Palmer Cox
Book cover
1896, U.S.A.
Lithograph

ARTIST: Unknown
Trade cards
Late 19th C., U.S.A.
Chromo lithographs

ARTIST: Unknown
Trade cards
Late 19th C., France
Chromo lithographs

CHICORÉE A LA BERGÈRE
EMILE BONZEL
HAUBOURDIN (NORD)

N° 4

LE CANARD. — Dites donc, il m'a été dit que la
mortalité allait en augmentant dans le pays, ce
n'est guère rassurant pour y venir habiter si c'est
dû à une épidémie qui court.
L'OIE. — Oh! oui, M'sieu, ça court!! c'est l'épidémie d'auto!!!

ARTIST: Unknown
Trade card
Late 19th C., France
Chromo lithograph

CAPTURED BY THE "DUDE".

THE "DUDE" MASHED.

ARTIST: Unknown
Trade cards
Late 19th C., U.S.A.
Chromo lithographs

ARTIST: Unknown
Trade card
Late 19th C., France
Chromo lithograph

Take a back seat, will I ? I'll let you know whom I'm glaring at.

THE GREAT ATLANTIC & PACIFIC TEA CO'S TEAS & COFFEES ARE THE BEST!

COPYRIGHT, 1883 BY THE GREAT ATLANTIC & PACIFIC TEA CO. N.Y.

Owl man and Owl woman, Owl maid and Owl bach, They are happy once more Tho' they've had many a scratch.

THE GREAT ATLANTIC & PACIFIC TEA CO'S TEAS & COFFEES ARE THE BEST!

Copyright, 1883, by the Great Atlantic & Pacific Tea Co.

ARTIST: Unknown
Trade cards
1883, U.S.A.
Chromo lithographs

ARTIST: Unknown
Trade card
Late 19th C., France
Chromo lithograph

COMMISSION RECEIVED.

ARTIST: Unknown
Trade card
Late 19th C., U.S.A.
Chromo lithograph

ARTIST: Unknown
Trade card
Late 19th C., France
Chromo lithograph

A LA PLACE CLICHY

ARTIST: Unknown
Trade card (trimmed)
Late 19th C., U.S.A.
Chromo lithograph

KASSELER HAFER-KAKAO

HAUSEN & C° KASSEL

SERIE 3.   N° 3.

KASSELER HAFER-KAKAO

HAUSEN & C° KASSEL

SERIE 3.   N° 6.

ARTIST: Unknown
Trade cards
Late 19th C., Germany
Chromo lithographs

ARTIST: Unknown
Trade card
Late 19th C., U.S.A.
Chromo lithograph

JAS. S. KIRK & CO.   SOAP MAKERS
CHICAGO.
"AMERICAN FAMILY"

ARTISTS: Unknown
Die cut scraps
Late 19th C., Unknown
Chromo lithographs

ARTISTS: Unknown
Die cut scraps
Late 19th C., Unknown
Chromo lithographs

Pigeon.

Quack Doctor.

Pretty Poll.

An old Hen.

Old Rooster.

ARTISTS: Unknown
Tobacco cards
1889, U.S.A.
Chromo lithographs

RESEMBLANCE.

A. RAYMOND & CO.
FASHIONABLE CLOTHIERS.

ARTIST: Unknown
Trade cards
Late 19th C., U.S.A.
Chromo lithograph

ARTIST: Unknown
Postcard
Late 19th C., U.S.A.
Offset lithograph

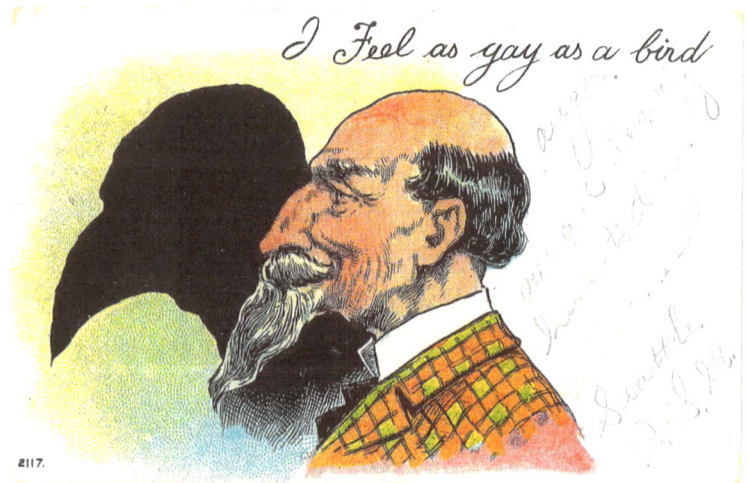

I Feel as gay as a bird

2117.

A SAINT JOSEPH
NOUVEAUTÉS

117-119, RUE MONTMARTRE, & 2, RUE JOQUELET
MARTIN PÊCHEUR

ARTIST: Unknown
Trade cards
Late 19th C., France
Chromo lithographs

ANNUAL SALE EIGHT MILLION JARS

FAISAN DORÉ

ARTIST: Unknown
Trade card
Late 19th C., France
Chromo lithograph

NATURAL HISTORY SERIES—BIRDS,

1508

"THE STORK"

HABITAT—BABYLAND.

COPYRIGHTED 1905 BY ULLMAN MFG.CO.N.Y.

ARTIST: Unknown
Postcard
1905, U.S.A.
Chromo lithograph

OLD ROOSTER.

You make pretense of being young,
Though your muscle's weak and nerves unstrung,
Your actions go from bad to worse
So you really ought to have a nurse.

COPYRIGHT 1907, BY THE ROSE COMPANY.

ARTIST: Unknown
Postcard
1907, U.S.A.
Offset lithograph

T'es bête comme une oie.

ARTIST: Unknown
Postcard
Late 19th C., France
Chromo lithograph

58. A Jay Bird

ARTIST: H. Martin
Postcard
Early 20th C., U.S.A.
Offset lithograph

A Joyous Easter

ARTIST: Unknown
Postcard
Early 20th C., Germany
Chromo lithograph

ARTIST: Unknown
Postcard
Early 20th C., Germany
Chromo lithograph

ARTIST: Unknown
Postcard
Early 20th C., U.S.A.
Chromo lithograph

ARTIST: Unknown
Postcard
Early 20th C., U.S.A.
Chromo lithograph

A YOUNG GOOSE.

ARTIST: Unknown
Postcard
Early 20th C., U.S.A.
Offset lithograph

CROWING AGAIN.

ARTIST: Unknown
Postcard
Early 20th C., U.S.A.
Offset lithograph

You are a Bird

ARTIST: Unknown
Postcard
Early 20th C., U.S.A.
Offset lithograph

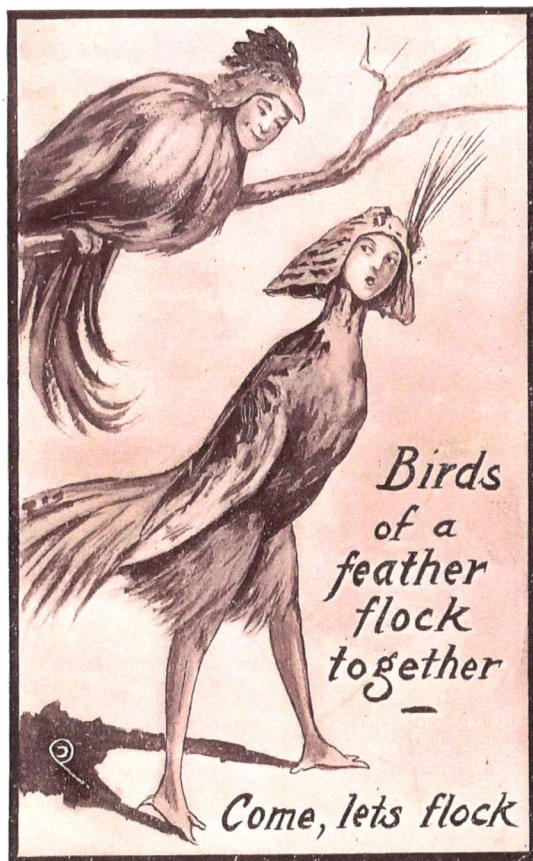

Birds of a feather flock together —

Come, lets flock

ARTIST: Unknown
Postcard
Early 20th C., U.S.A.
Offset lithograph

ARTIST: J.S. Pughe
Magazine cover
1904, U.S.A.
Chromo lithograph

PRETTY POLL!

THE BIRD-FANCIER. — Talk? Say, he's as good as a phonograph!

ARTIST: Joseph Keppler
Magazine illustration
1906, U.S.A.
Chromo lithograph

Chantecler

In 1910 French playwright, Edmond Rostand (1868-1918), best known for his play *Cyrano de Bergerac*, presented the satirical play *Chantecler*. The play, who's main character is a barn-yard rooster, included an entire cast costumed mostly in avian animal suits.

ARTIST: A. Edel
Costume Design
1908, France
Offset

ARTIST: Georges Scott
Magazine illustration
1910, France
Offset

ARTIST: A. Edel
Costume Designs
1908, France
Offset

CHANTECLER, DE M. EDMOND ROSTAND

P. LORSY, LA POULE GRISE   DERÉVAL, LA POULE HOUDAN

CHANTECLER

ARTIST: Bert
Postcard
1910 France
Photographic Offset

ARTIST: Unknown
Postcard
1912 France
Offset

CATS

When the cat's away the mice will play.

Old Proverb

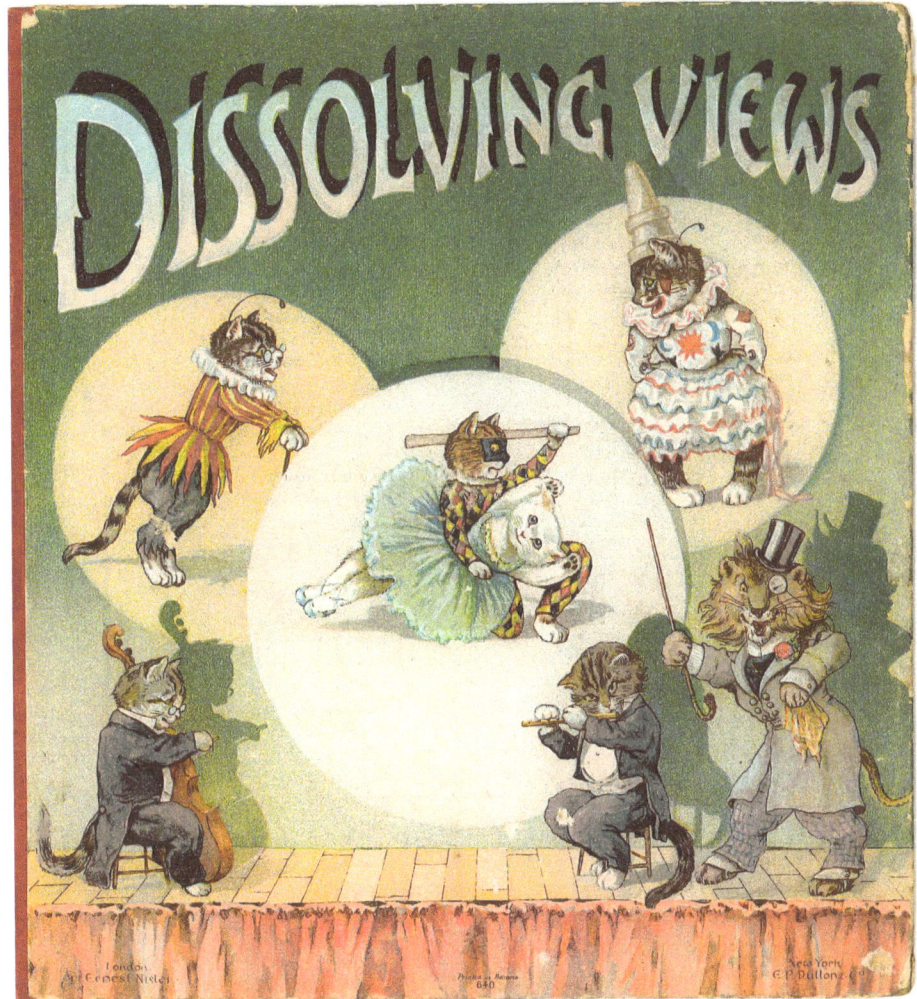

ARTIST: Unknown
Book cover
Date unknown
Chromo lithograph

ARTIST: John Tenniel
Magazine illustrations
1887, England
Engraving

The 3 Little Kittens.

Mounted on Linen. Pleasewell Series.

Copyrighted 1890. by McLoughlin Bro's NEW-YORK.

ARTIST: Unknown
Book cover
1890, U.S.A.
Chromo lithograph

ARTIST:
Charles H. Bennett
Book illustration
1857, England
Hand colored engraving

ARTIST: Unknown
Book illustration
Date unknown, U.S.A.
Chromo lithograph

ONE POUND CHESTS. HALF POUND CHESTS.

JUNGLE CHOP FORMOSA TEA.

ARTIST: Unknown
Trade card
Date unknown, U.S.A.
Chromo lithograph

PERFORMING CATS

ARTIST: Unknown
Trade card
Date unknown, U.S.A.
Chromo lithograph

ARTIST: Unknown
Die cut scrap
Date unknown
Chromo lithograph

ARTIST: Unknown
Trade card
1888, U.S.A.
Chromo lithograph

ARTIST: Unknown
Die cut scrap
Date unknown
Chromo lithograph

ARTIST: Unknown
Trade card
Late 19th C., U.S.A.
Lithograph

ARTIST: Unknown
Trade card
Late 19th C., U.S.A.
Lithograph

ARTIST: Unknown
Trade card
Late 19th C., U.S.A.
Lithograph

ARTIST: Unknown
Trade card
1881, U.S.A.
Lithograph

GREATLY IMPROVED FOR 1881
THE ADAMS & WESTLAKE, WIRE GAUZE, NON EXPLOSIVE, OIL STOVE.

WIRE GAUZE   THE ADAMS & WESTLAKE NON EXPLOSIVE

A MARVEL OF COMFORT & CONVENIENCE.

87

A strong Lion.

The Tiger.

A cat nap.

ARTIST: Unknown
Tobacco Cards
1889, U.S.A.
Chromo lithograph

ARTIST: Unknown
Trade card
Late 19th C., France
Chromo lithograph

NOLAN BROS.   FINE SHOES.

PHELAN BUILDING.   SAN FRANCISCO.

ARTIST: Unknown
Die cut scraps
Late 19th C.
Chromo lithograph

ARTIST: Unknown
Trade card
Late 19th C., U.S.A.
Chromo lithograph

ARTIST: Unknown
Trade card
Late 19th C., France
Chromo lithograph

FAIRBANK CANNING CO.

COOKED CORNED BEEF,   CHICAGO, ILL.

WE LEAD ALL COMPETITORS.

ARTIST: Unknown
Trade card
Late 19th C., U.S.A.
Chromo lithograph

ARTIST: Unknown
Die cuts
Late 19th C.
Chromo lithograph

ARTIST: Unknown
Die cut scrap
Late 19th C.
Chromo lithograph

ARTIST: Unknown
Die cut scrap
Late 19th C.
Chromo lithograph

Puss in Boots

ARTIST: Unknown
Die cut scraps
Late 19th C.
Chromo lithographs

ARTIST: Unknown
Die cut scrap
Late 19th C.
Chromo lithograph

ARTIST: Unknown
Trade card
Late 19th C., U.S.A.
Chromo lithograph

And Mother Puss said, "Now its no use to cry.
If you don't find your mittens I'll give you no pie."

ARTIST: Unknown
Die cut scrap
Late 19th C.
Chromo lithograph

ARTIST: Unknown
Die cut scrap
Late 19th C.
Chromo lithograph

GRANDMA'S PET

BUY HEEKIN'S MANILLA COFFEE
That has the strength of Rio, and Java flavor
OR WHITE CAP BAKING POWDER
¼lb. can for 5c., and get a beautiful picture.
JAS. HEEKIN & CO., CINCINNATI.

"I HA DA DARLING RACKET LAST NIGHT"

Compliments of
◁RAMSDELL'S▷
99 CENT STORE,
No. 0 Wilson's Block,   No. Adams, Mass.

ARTIST: Unknown
Trade cards
Late 19th C., U.S.A.
Lithographs

ARTIST: Unknown
Trade cards
Late 19th C., U.S.A.
Chromo lithographs

USE
KAZINE
YOUR GROCER SELLS IT.   (OVER)

How terribly lonesome I feel? How queer,
To be sitting alone, with nobody near,
Oh how I wish Maria was here.
                              Mon dieu!
The thought of it fills me with horrible doubt,
I should smile, I should blush, I should wail, I should shout,
Just suppose some fellow has cut me out!
                              Me out!

Dr. Morse's Indian Root Pills.

The Best Family Pill in use.

FOR SALE EVERYWHERE.

Ah, there she comes now, as soft as a rat!
But alas, he'd mistaken the soft pit-a-pat,
His Maria was only a brother tom-cat.
                              "How's that!"
Thought Tom No.1, of Tom No.2,
But No.2 bounced him without more ado,
And suddenly both departed from view.
                              Mew, mew!

Dr. Morse's Indian Root Pills.

The Best Family Pill in use.

FOR SALE EVERYWHERE.

ARTIST: Unknown
Trade cards
Late 19th C., U.S.A.
Chromo lithographs

USE
KAZINE.
YOUR GROCER SELLS IT.   (OVER)

A. W. Bolland

COPYRIGHTED 1881, BY J.C. BEARD.

ARTIST: Unknown
Trade card
1881, U.S.A.
Chromo lithograph

122
A

Darling has your
love grown cold.

Tobin
N.Y.

ARTIST: Tobin
Trade card
Late 19th C., U.S.A.
Chromo lithograph

ARTIST: Unknown
Trade card
Late 19th C., U.S.A.
Chromo lithograph

DID YOU SEE ME GET THE BEST OF HIM?

Copyright by A.B. Seeley 188?

ARTIST: Unknown
Trade card
Late 19th C., U.S.A.
Chromo lithograph

Though little Willie has got in trouble, He is as happy as a big Soap bubble.

B 316

ARTIST: Unknown
Trade card
Late 19th C., U.S.A.
Chromo lithograph

Ye Grand Ballet.
In which
Mdsle Tom Cat does
the great Toe Act.

ARTIST: Unknown
Trade card
Late 19th C., U.S.A.
Chromo lithograph

ARTIST: Unknown
Trade card
1881, U.S.A.
Chromo lithograph

COPYRIGHTED 1881 BY J.C. BEARD

ARTIST: Unknown
Trade cards
1881, U.S.A.
Chromo lithograph

THE LOTTERY.
TOMMY NEGOTIATING FOR A TICKET.

COPYRIGHT 1884 BY A.H. SMITH

ARTIST: Unknown
Trade card
Late 19th C., U.S.A.
Chromo lithograph

THE 1ST PRIZE.
THE VERY IMAGE OF ITS FATHER.

COPYRIGHT 1882 BY A. M. SMITH

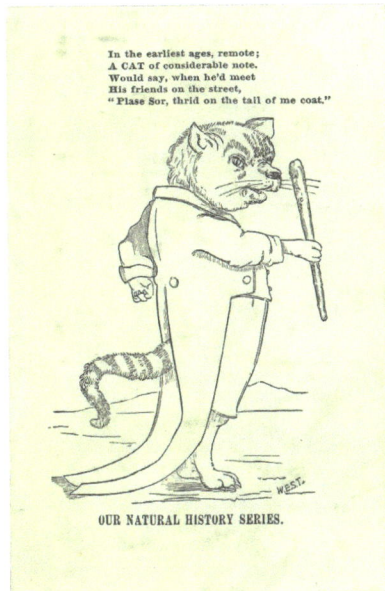

In the earliest ages, remote;
A CAT of considerable note.
Would say, when he'd meet
His friends on the street,
"Plase Sor, thrid on the tail of me coat."

OUR NATURAL HISTORY SERIES.

ARTIST: Unknown
Trade card
1881, U.S.A.
Chromo lithograph

ARTIST: W.E.S.T.
Trade card
Late 19th C., U.S.A.
Chromo lithograph

ARTIST: Unknown
Post card
Early 20th C., U.S.A.
Chromo lithograph

ARTIST: Unknown
Post card
Early 20th C., Germany
Chromo lithograph

ARTIST: Unknown
Post card
Early 20th C., U.S.A.
Chromo lithograph

You Auto See Us

An Easter Hymn April 23. 1915

ARTIST: Unknown
Post card
Early 20th C., France
Chromo lithograph

Just Cats!
Ere long, his love he did declare,
And begged in marriage pussy fair.

ARTIST: Unknown
Post card
Early 20th C., U.S.A.
Offset

To my Sweet Valentine

ARTIST: Unknown
Post card
Early 20th C., U.S.A.
Chromo lithograph

"It's not my face, kid,
it's my shape"

ARTIST: Unknown
Post card
Early 20th C., U.S.A.
Offset

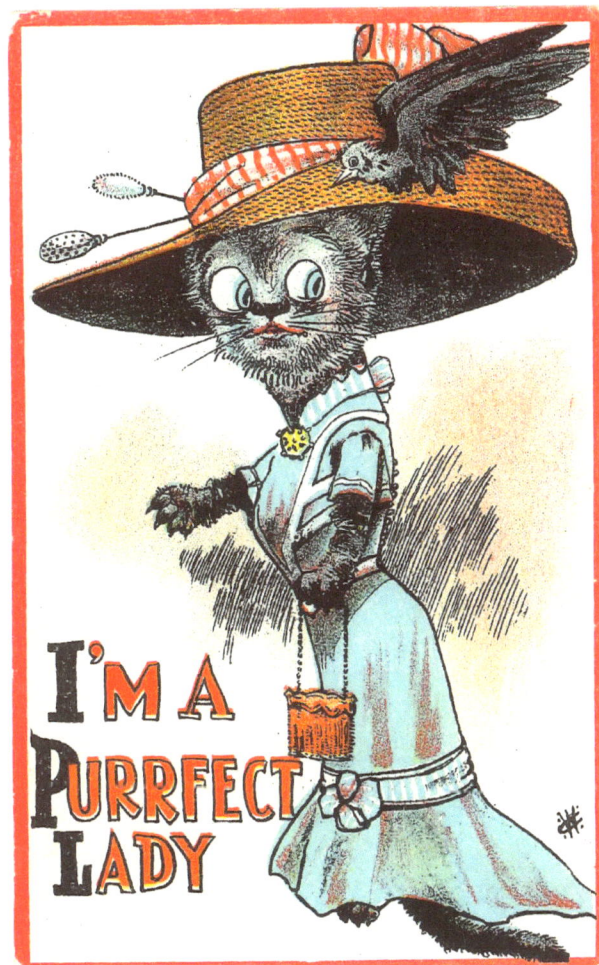

I'M A PURRFECT LADY

ARTIST: Unknown
Post card
Early 20th C., U.S.A.
Lithograph

DOGS, WOLVES AND FOXES

"You cannot recognize people by their clothes, nor dogs by their coats."
15th Century saying

Take warning hence, ye children fair; of wolves' insidious arts beware; And as you pass each lonely wood, Ah! think of small Red-riding-hood.
Red Riding Hood, Anonymous. 1801

"Suspicion all our lives shall be stuck full of eyes; for treason is but trusted like the fox."
Shakespeare, King Henry IV, Part 1

Copyrighted 1880 by Chas. Brown.

ARTIST: Levilly
Book illustration
Mid 19th Century, France
Hand colored lithograph

Levilly

Lith. de Villain.

ARTIST: Charles H. Bennett
Book illustration
1857, England
Hand colored lithograph

ARTIST: M.B. De Monvel
Book illustration
1893, France
Chromo lithograph

Un loup n'avait que les os et la peau,
Tant les chiens faisaient bonne garde :
Ce loup rencontre un dogue aussi puissant que beau,

Gras, poli, qui s'était fourvoyé par mégarde.
L'attaquer, le mettre en quartiers,
Sire loup l'eût fait volontiers :
Mais il fallait livrer bataille ;

Et le mâtin était de taille
A se défendre hardiment.
Le loup donc l'aborde humblement,

Entre en propos, et lui fait compliment
Sur son embonpoint, qu'il admire.

« Il ne tiendra qu'à vous, beau sire,
D'être aussi gras que moi, lui repartit le chien.
Quittez les bois, vous ferez bien :
Vos pareils y sont misérables,

Cancres, hères, et pauvres diables,
Dont la condition est de mourir de faim.
Car, quoi ! rien d'assuré ! point de franche lippée !
Tout à la pointe de l'épée !
Suivez-moi, vous aurez un bien meilleur destin. »

ARTIST: Bernard Gillam
Magazine illustration
1885, U.S.A.
Chromo lithograph

ARTIST: John Karst
Book illustrations
1869, U.S.A.
Chromo lithographs

THE EVENING WALK.

Look at this high and mighty pair,
Two dogs of grave and stately air —
My Lord, with cane and nice cravat,
And shining hat a-top of that,
Walks loftily, while like a bride
My lady trips in silken pride.
Tom slyly joins their promenade.
While Joe the page, with footsteps staid
And jacket laced with shining braid,
Struts on behind with gold cockade.

ARTIST: Unknown
Book illustration
1883, U.S.A.
Chromo lithograph

THE DOGGIE'S PROMENADE

Saalfield's Muslin Books
"EVER WEAR-NEVER TEAR"

Mrs. DAVID A. MUNRO.

COPYRIGHT 1907 BY
THE SAALFIELD PUBLISHING CO.,
NEW YORK ~ AKRON, OHIO ~ CHICAGO

ARTIST: Unknown
Book cover
1907, U.S.A.
Offset

ARTIST: Unknown
Magazine illustration
1887, England
Engraving

ARTIST: Unknown
Jigsaw puzzle
Late 19th C., U.S.A.
Chromo lithograph

RED RIDING HOOD
COPYRIGHT, 1884, WOOLSON SPICE CO.
SEE STORY ON OTHER SIDE

ARTIST: Unknown
Trade card
1884, U.S.A.
Chromo lithograph

ARTIST: Unknown
Trade card
Late 19th C., U.S.A.
Chromo lithograph

ARTIST: Unknown
Book illustration
Late 19th C., U.S.A.
Chromo lithograph

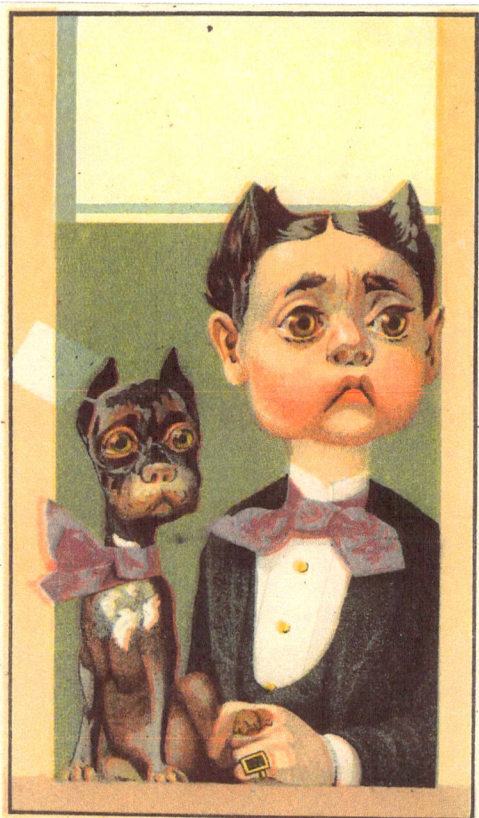

ARTIST: Unknown
Trade cards
Late 19th C., U.S.A.
Chromo lithographs

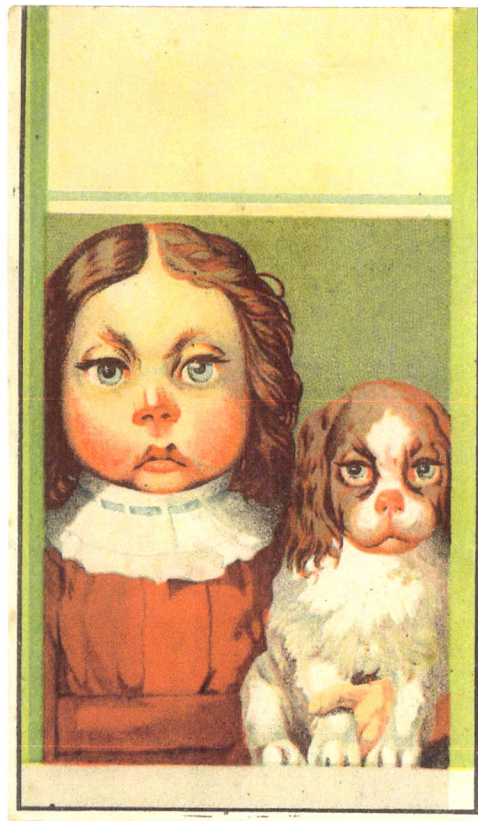

ARTIST: Unknown
Trade card
Late 19th C., U.S.A.
Chromo lithograph

COMPLIMENTS OF
R. FITZGERALD,
DEALER IN
BOOTS, SHOES & RUBBERS,
Gents' Fine Custom Boots and Shoes a Specialty.
270 State Street,   Rochester, N. Y.

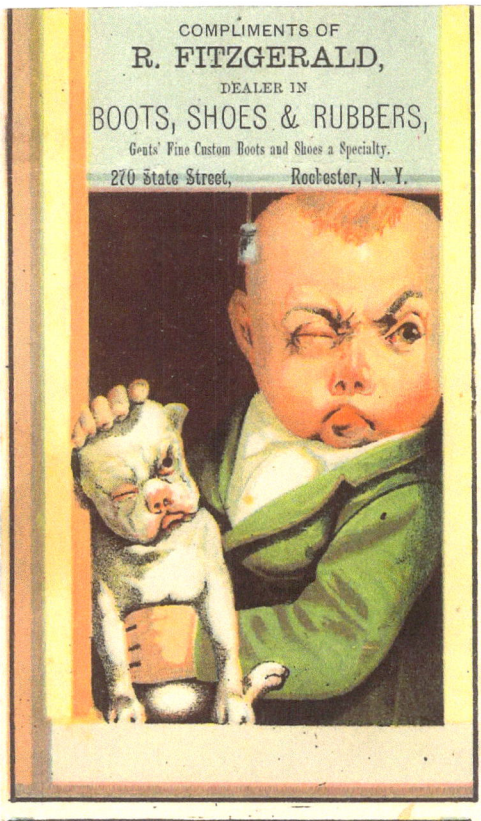

ARTIST: Unknown
Die cut
Late 19th C., U.S.A.
Chromo lithograph

OH! GEVUS A REST.
COPYRIGHTED, BUFFORD, BOSTON.
MRS. DINSMORE'S
COUGH AND CROUP BALSAM
CURES
a COUGH in One Day
and the CROUP in One Minute

A GIRL OF THE PERIOD.

P. J. FLANNERY,
FINE SHOES,
ODD FELLOWS' BUILDING,
Marysville, Cal.

ARTIST: Unknown
Trade cards
Late 19th C., U.S.A.
Lithographs

BOVRIL

BOVRIL

ARTIST: Unknown
Trade cards
Late 19th C., France
Chromo lithographs

122
A

We never speak
as we pass by.

Her bright smile
haunts me still

122
A

ARTIST: Tobin
Trade cards
Late 19th C., U.S.A.
Lithographs

Jos. Figel & Son.
Merchant Tailors
And Importers of
Gents' and Boys'
CLOTHING
Furnishing Goods,
Neckwear, etc.
211 Montgomery St.
Russ House Block.
San Francisco, Cal.

ARTIST: Unknown
Trade card
Late 19th C., U.S.A.
Lithograph

ARTIST: Unknown
Die cut
Late 19th C., Germany
Chromo lithograph

To My Valentine

in Germany

ARTIST: Unknown
Die cut
Late 19th Century
Chromo lithograph

ARTIST: Unknown
Trade card
Late 19th C., U.S.A.
Lithograph

CROMPTON'S
CORALINE
CORSET.

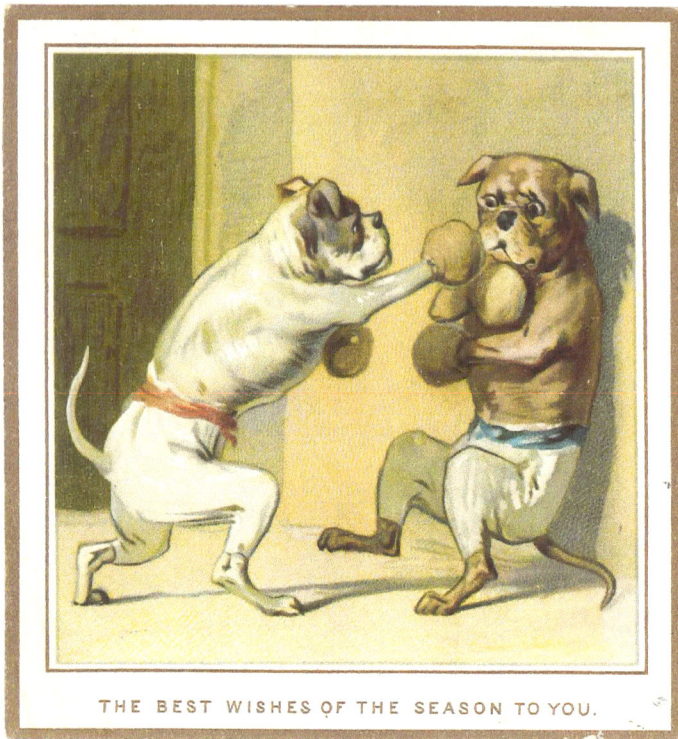

ARTIST: Unknown
Cigarette card
Late 19th C.
Chromo lithograph

ARTIST: Unknown
Die cut
Late 19th C.
Chromo lithograph

THE BEST WISHES OF THE SEASON TO YOU.

ARTIST: Unknown
Die cut
Late 19th C.
Chromo lithograph

ARTIST: Unknown
Die cut
Late 19th C.
Chromo lithograph

ARTIST: Unknown
Die cut
Late 19th C.
Chromo lithograph

ARTIST: Unknown
Cigarette card
Late 19th C.
Chromo lithograph

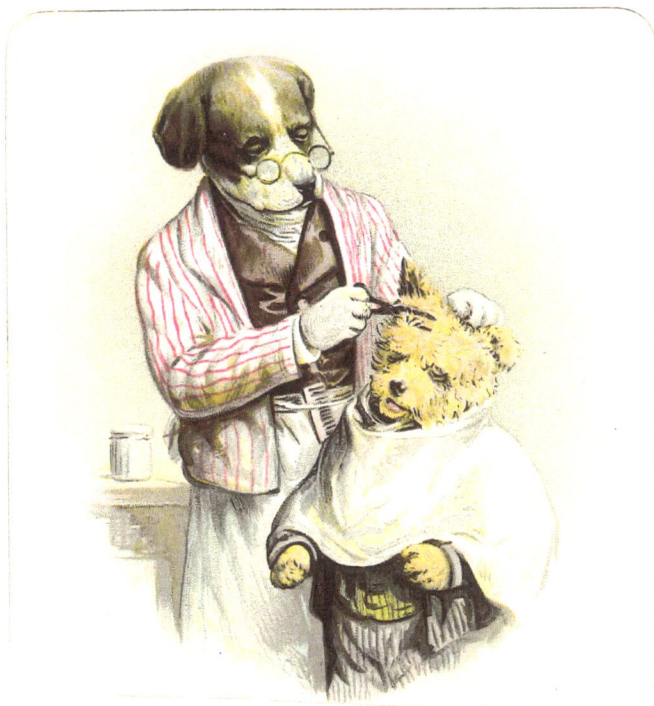

ARTIST: Unknown
Cigarette card
Late 19th C.
Chromo lithograph

ALLEN & GINTER'S
PET
CIGARETTES
are the best.

ARTIST: Unknown
Die cut
Late 19th C.
Chromo lithograph

ARTIST: Unknown
Die cut
Late 19th C.
Chromo lithograph

BEAU'S RESTAURANT,
No. 3 West 14th Street, New York.

ARTIST: Unknown
Trade cards
Late 19th C., U.S.A.
Chromo lithographs

ARTIST: Unknown
Die cut
Late 19th C.
Chromo lithograph

ARTIST: Unknown
Die cut
Late 19th C.
Chromo lithograph

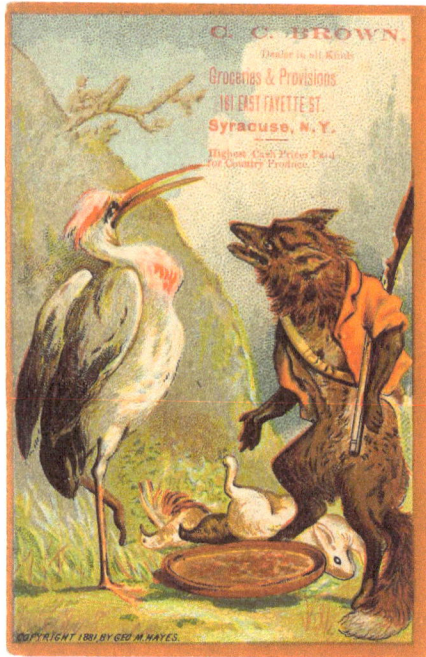

ARTIST: Unknown
Trade cards
Late 19th C., U.S.A.
Chromo lithographs

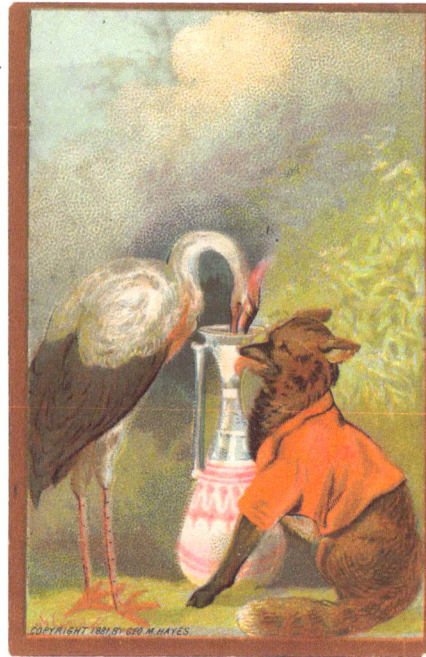

ARTIST: Unknown
Die cut
Late 19th C.
Chromo lithograph

ARTIST: Unknown
Die cut
Late 19th C.
Chromo lithograph

ARE
YOU
THERE?

Most useful thing is a telephone—
"Hello, Mr. Butcher, I want a bone!"

ARTIST: W. Foster
Book illustration
1907, England
Offset

ARTIST: Unknown
Post card
Late 19th C., Germany
Chromo lithograph

Une surprise.

Ser. 6.   384

ARTIST: Unknown
Post card
Late 19th C., Germany
Chromo lithograph

It's simply a dog's life
when you're single

ARTIST: Wall
Post card
Early 20th C., U.S.A.
Lithograph

TOO MONGREL FOR THE BENCH SHOW

ARTIST: Unknown
Post card
Early 20th C., U.S.A.
Lithograph

ARTIST: Unknown
Post card
Late 19th C., Germany
Chromo lithograph

ARTIST: Unknown
Post card
Late 19th C., Germany
Chromo lithograph

2187   BEGORRA!

ARTIST: Wall
Post card
Early 20th C., U.S.A.
Offset

ARTIST: Unknown
Post card
Early 20th C., France
Offset

Tu bois sans cesse et
te grises chaque jour,
A faire des enfants tu
t'appliques toujours.
Ton profil d'animal
n'est pas un hasard,
Car les petits que tu fais,
sont des petits renards.

ARTIST: Unknown
Post card
Late 19th C., France
Chromo lithograph

ARTIST: Unknown
Post card
Late 19th C., Germany
Chromo lithograph

ARTIST: Unknown
Post card
Late 19th C., Germany
Chromo lithograph

ARTIST: Unknown
Post card
Late 19th C., France
Chromo lithograph

Tryin' to be good.

Simply feelin' bully.

ARTIST: Unknown
Post cards
Early 20th C., U.S.A.
Offset

When this you see —
then think of me!

Made several attempts to write but haven't succeeded yet.

PIGS

The pig in sheer gluttony spares not even its own young.

Aelian
Third Century AD

ARTIST: Walter Browne
Magazine illustration detail
1887, England
Engraving

ARTIST: Unknown
Book illustration
Unknown, U.S.A.
Woodcut

Piggy goes for a Wig.

WHERE are you going to, you little pig?
"I'm going to the Barber's to buy me a wig!"
A wig, little pig!
A pig in a wig!
Why, who ever before saw a pig in a wig?

ARTIST: Saalburg
Newspaper illustration
1891, U.S.A.
Lithograph

ARTIST: Unknown
Book illustration
1915, England
Halftone lithograph

It pays to keep posted
regarding UTICA. ❧ ❧

No. 56

ARTIST: Unknown
Trade card
Late 19th C., U.S.A.
Chromo lithograph

"AGRICULTURAL FURNACE & BOILER."

ARTIST: Unknown
Trade card
Late 19th C., U.S.A.
Chromo lithograph

FAMILIAR QUOTATIONS
AS APPLIED BY
N. K. FAIRBANK & CO.
LARD REFINERS.

Why do those Cliffs of shadowy tint, appear
More sweet than all the water that is near?
It is not distance makes the view enchanting,
But home, and Fairbank's Lard, that I am wanting.
(Campbell, Pleasures of Hope.)

FAMILIAR QUOTATIONS
AS APPLIED BY
N. K. FAIRBANK & CO.
LARD REFINERS.

Go get some Lard, and let some Lard be got,
And let the one who gets it be a getter,
For if he gets Fairbank's pure Lard, he'll not,
No, never in his life find any better.
(Henry Carey, Mock Heroics.)

ARTISTS: Unknown
Trade cards
Late 19th C., U.S.A.
Lithograph

ARTISTS: Unknown
Die cuts
Late 19th C.
Chromo lithograph

LUNATICS, ALL OF YOU! CRAZY TO GET INTO FAIRBANK & Co. LARD TANK

IN THAT OUR CHIEF HAPPINESS CONSISTS.

OUR BACHELORS

ARTIST: Unknown
Trade card
Late 19th C., U.S.A.
Lithograph

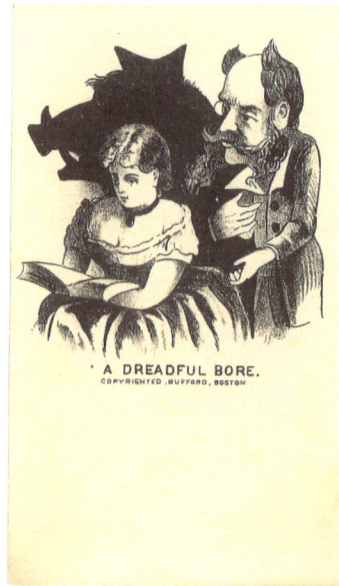

A DREADFUL BORE.
COPYRIGHTED .BUFFORD, BOSTON

ARTIST: Unknown
Trade card
Late 19th C., U.S.A.
Lithograph

ARTIST: Unknown
Trade card
1877, U.S.A.
Chromo lithograph

Yours for Good Luck

ARTIST: Unknown
Greeting Card
Early 20th C., U.S.A.
Offset

MAGNOLIA
IS KING OF ALL HAMS

138

ARTIST: Unknown
Postcard
Early 20th C., Germany
Chromo lithograph

En glad jul!

ARTIST: Jenni Nistron (?)
Postcard
Early 20th C., Sweden
Chromo lithograph

ARTIST: Unknown
Postcard
Early 20th C., Germany
Lithograph

Prosit Neujahr!

ARTIST: Unknown
Postcard
Early 20th C., Germany
Offset

To My Valentine

Laugh and the world laughs with you

ARTIST: Arthur Thiele
Postcards
Early 20th C., Germany
Offset

ARTIST: Unknown
Postcard
Early 20th C., Germany
Lithograph

ARTIST: Unknown
Postcard
Early 20th C., Germany
Lithograph

ARTIST: Unknown
Postcard
Early 20th C., Germany
Chromo lithograph

ARTIST: Unknown
Postcard
Late 19th C., Germany
Lithograph

ARTIST: Unknown
Postcard
Late 19th C., Germany
Chromo lithograph

ARTIST: Unknown
Postcard
Late 19th C., Germany
Chromo lithograph

ARTIST: Unknown
Postcard
Early 20th C., Germany
Offset

ARTIST: O. Weise
Postcard
Early 20th C., Netherlands
Offset

BEARS AND BULLS

"Arts and sciences are not cast in a mold, but formed and perfected by degrees, by often handling and polishing, as bears leisurely lick their cubs into form."

Michel de Montaigne

"A mingled form where two strange shapes combined, And different nature, bull and man, where joined."

Euripides

ARTIST: Unknown
Tobacco card
Late 19th C., U.S.A.
Chromo lithograph

ARTIST: Unknown
Tobacco card
Late 19th C., U.S.A.
Chromo lithograph

1er Avril!

Quand on veut plaire et qu'on est vieux,
Faut avoir une grosse bourse
Avec ça on peut être gâteux
Et pas plus aimable qu'un ours.

ARTIST: Unknown
Postcard
Late 19th C., France
Chromo lithograph

Marshall & Ball.
CLOTHIERS.
807 809 & 811 Broad St.
NEWARK, N. J.

A "Bear."

ARTIST: Unknown
Trade card
Late 19th C., U.S.A.
Chromo lithograph

WHITE, BLACK AND COLORS FOR HAND & MACHINE

ARTIST: Unknown
Trade card
1887, U.S.A.
Chromo lithograph

BUSY BEARS—VACATION.

COPYRIGHT BY J. I. AUSTEN CO., CHICAGO.—438

BUSY BEARS—PLAYING LEAP FROG.

COPYRIGHT BY J. I. AUSTEN CO., CHICAGO.—434

ARTIST: Unknown
Postcards
Early 20th C., U.S.A.
Offset

I'm not going anywhere
I am coming back

246

stuck again

249

ARTIST: Unknown
Postcards
Early 20th, U.S.A.
Offset

THE CAKE WALK.

THE JOLLY ANGLERS.

ARTIST: Unknown
Postcards
Early 20th, England
Offset

JOHN BULL, Dr. Busby's Butcher.

PATTY BULL, The Butcher's Daughter.

ARTIST: Unknown
Game Cards
Late 19th C., U.S.A.
Chromo lithographs

ARTIST: Unknown
Die cut Scrap
Late 19th C.,
Chromo lithograph

I'm a young man from the country.

DETROIT MUSIC CO.,
184 & 186 WOODWARD AVE.

ARTIST: Tobin
Trade card
Late 19th C., U.S.A.
Lithograph

ARTIST: Tobin
Trade card
Late 19th C., U.S.A.
Lithograph

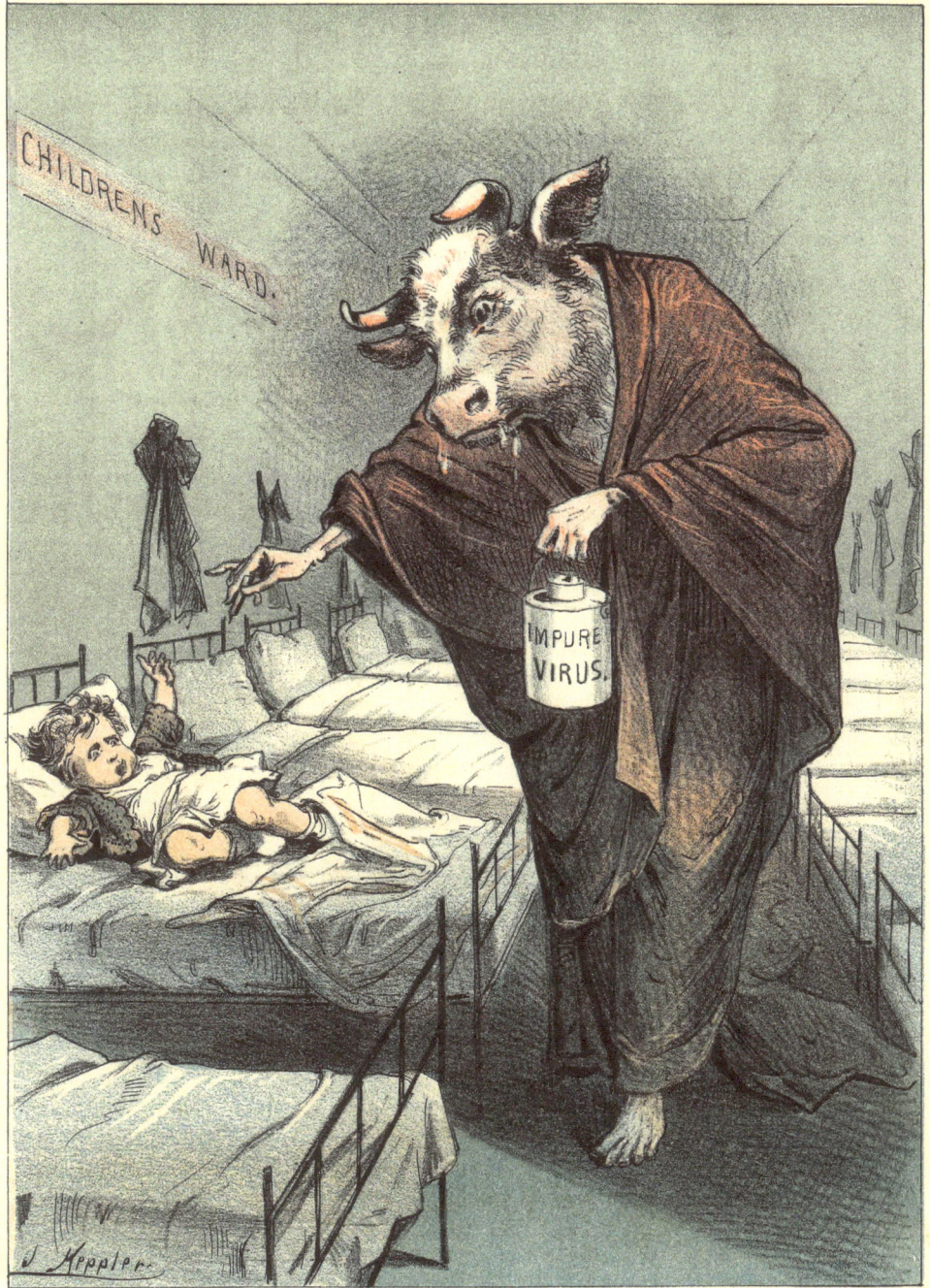

ARTIST: Joseph Keppler
Magazine Illustration
Late 19th C., U.S.A.
Lithograph

RABBITS

"Alice started to her feet, for it flashed across her mind that she had never before seen a rabbit with either a waist-coat-pocket, or a watch to take out of it, and burning with curiosity, she ran across the field after it, and was just in time to see it pop down a large rabbit-hole under the hedge."

Lewis Carroll
Alice's Adventures in Wonderland

BUNNY BUN

ARTIST: Unknown
Game Cards
Late 19th C., U.S.A.
Chromo lithograph

LUNCHEON BEEF.

· READY · FOR · TABLE · USE ·

ARTIST: Unknown
Trade cards
Late 19th C., U.S.A.
Chromo lithographs

ARTIST: Unknown
Die cut scrap
Late 19th C.
Chromo lithograph

ARTIST: Unknown
Die cut scrap
Late 19th C.
Chromo lithograph

R. L. BERRY,
PIANOS AND ORGANS
SPRINGFIELD, ILL.

ARTIST: Unknown
Trade card
Late 19th C., U.S.A.
Chromo lithograph

C. CURTIN,
GRAND DRY GOODS STORE,

911 and 913 Market Street,
San Francisco, Cal.

SUNSHINE PUB. CO. PHILA.

ARTIST: Unknown
Trade card
Late 19th C., U.S.A.
Chromo lithograph

Fröhliche OSTERN

ARTIST: Unknown
Die cut scrap
Late 19th C., Germany
Chromo lithograph

157

ARTIST: Unknown
Trade card
Late 19th C., France
Chromo lithograph

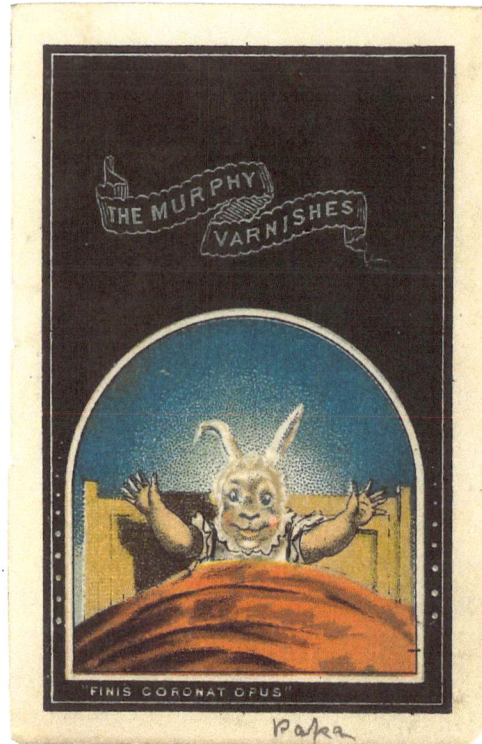

ARTIST: Unknown
Trade card
Late 19th C., France
Chromo lithograph

ARTIST: Unknown
Die cut scrap
Late 19th C.
Chromo lithograph

ARTIST: Unknown
Die cut scraps
Early 20th C.
Offset

ARTIST: Unknown
Postcard
Early 20th C., U.S.A.
Chromo lithograph

ARTIST: Unknown
Postcard
Early 20th C., Germany
Chromo lithograph

ARTIST: Unknown
Postcard
Early 20th C., Germany
Chromo lithograph

ARTIST: Unknown
Postcard
Early 20th C., Germany
Chromo lithograph

Easter Greetings.

ARTIST: Unknown
Postcard
Early 20th C., Germany
Chromo lithograph

Easter Greetings

ARTIST: Unknown
Postcard
Early 20th C., Germany
Chromo lithograph

ARTIST: Unknown
Postcard
Early 20th C., Germany
Chromo lithograph

ARTIST: Unknown
Postcard
Early 20th C., Germany
Chromo lithograph

Easter Joys be Thine

Olive.

ARTIST: Unknown
Postcard
Early 20th C., U.S.A.
Chromo lithograph

Hauskaa Pääsiäistä

ARTIST: Unknown
Postcard
Early 20th C., Finland
Chromo lithograph

HORSES, MULES AND

A dishonest Groom used regularly to sell a good half of the measure of oats that was daily allowed for a horse, the care of which was intrusted to him. He would, however, keep currying the animal for hours together, to make him appear in good condition. The Horse naturally resented this treatment. "If you really wish me to look sleek," said he, "in future give me half the currying and leave off selling half my food."

Aesop

A Mule, well fed and worked but little, frisked and gamboled about in the fields, and said to himself, "What strength, what spirits are mine! My father must surely have been a thoroughbred Horse." He soon after fell into the hands of another master, and was worked hard and but scantily fed. Thoroughly jaded, he now said, "What could I have been thinking about the other day? I feel certain now that my father can only have been an Ass."

Aesop

DONKEYS

An Ass, finding a Lion's skin, put it on, and ranged about the forest. The Beasts fled in terror, and he was delighted at the success of his disguise. Meet a Fox, he rushed upon him, and this time he tried to imitate as well the roaring of the Lion. "Ah," said the Fox, "if you had held your tongue I should have been deceived like the rest; but now you bray I know who you are."

Aesop

ARTIST: Unknown
Trade card
Late 19th C., U.S.A.
Chromo lithograph

Peek Ah Boo!

ARTIST: Tobin
Trade card
Late 19th C., U.S.A.
Lithograph

CHEW MULE EAR FINE CUT.

WHAT THOUGH THE WORLD BE DARK AND DREAR,
YOUR HAPPY, IF YOU CHEW "MULE EAR"
MANUFACTURED BY
THE WELLMAN & DWIRE TOBACCO CO.
QUINCY, ILL.

THE CALVERT LITH. CO. DETROIT.

ARTIST: Unknown
Trade card
Late 19th C., U.S.A.
Lithograph

ARTIST: Unknown
Die cut scrap
Late 19th C.
Chromo lithograph

ARTIST: Unknown
Die cut scrap
Late 19th C.
Chromo lithograph

ARTIST: Unknown
Trade card
Late 19th C., U.S.A.
Lithograph

ARTIST: Unknown
Postcard
Early 20th C., U.S.A.
Offset

AN ANIMAL FAMOUS FOR ITS BRAY

January 1st, 1875.

S. Clark Rowlson.

ARTIST: Unknown
New Year's Card
1875
Chromo lithograph

ARTIST: Unknown
Die cut scrap
Late 19th C.
Chromo lithograph

ARTIST: Thomas Nast
Magazine Illustration
1881, U.S.A.
Offset

UNMASKED.

ARTIST: Klaus
Newspaper illustration
1896, U.S.A.
Offset

ARTIST: J.S. Pughe
Magazine illustration
1907, U.S.A.
Offset

170

ARTIST: Unknown
Postcard
Early 20th C., U.S.A.
Offset

MICE AND RATS

Hiccory, diccory, dock.
The mouse ran up the clock.
The clock struck one,
and down he run,
Hiccory, diccory, dock.

Mother Goose

"And out of the houses
the rats came tumbling.
Great rats, lean rats,
brawny rats,
Brown rats, black rats,
gray rats, tawny rats…"

Robert Browning
*The Pied Piper
of Hamelin*

ARTIST: Unknown
Handmade card
Early 20th C.
Ink and watercolor

ARTIST: Unknown
Trade cards
Late 19th C., U.S.A.
Chromo lithographs

ARTIST: Unknown
Handmade card
Early 20th C.
Ink and watercolor

A happy new Year.

174

ARTIST: Unknown
Trade card
Late 19th C., U.S.A.
Lithograph

ARTIST: Unknown
Trade cards
1881, U.S.A.
Lithographs

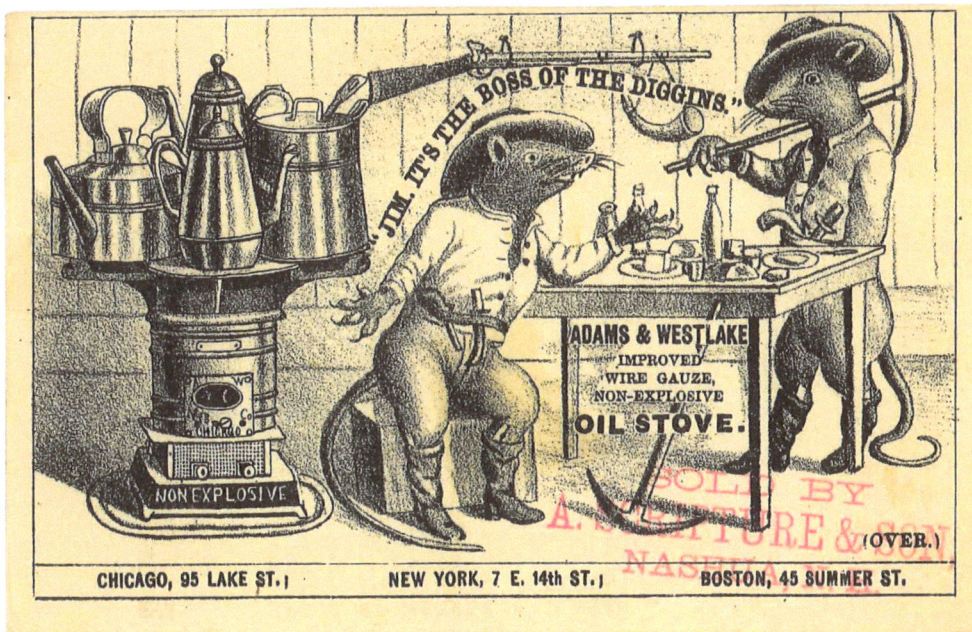

ARTIST: Unknown
Trade card
Late 19th C., U.S.A.
Lithograph

ARTIST: Unknown
Trade card
1881, U.S.A.
Chromo lithograph

FROGS

A Frog he would a-wooing go,
Whether his mother would let him
or no.

Anonymous

ARTIST: Unknown
Book illustration
1894, U.S.A.
Chromo lithograph

ARTIST: Palmer Cox
Calendar page
Early 20th C., U.S.A.
Offset

ARTIST: Unknown
Book illustration
Late 19th C., U.S.A.
Chromo lithograph

THORBURN'S.

The First Suit of Clothes.

(OVER.)

THORBURN'S.

The First Pipe.

(OVER.)

ARTIST: Unknown
Trade cards
Late 19th C., U.S.A.
Chromo lithographs

ARTIST: Unknown
Die cut scrap
Late 19th C., U.S.A.
Chromo lithograph

THORBURN'S.

The First Music Lesson.

(OVER.)

PROVIDENCE FURNITURE CO.,
BROAD ST., NEAR MATHEWSON.
(OVER)

ARTIST: Unknown
Die cut scrap
Late 19th C., U.S.A.
Chromo lithograph

ARTIST: Unknown
Trade card
Late 19th C., U.S.A.
Chromo lithograph

ARTIST: Unknown
Trade card
Late 19th C., U.S.A.
Chromo lithograph

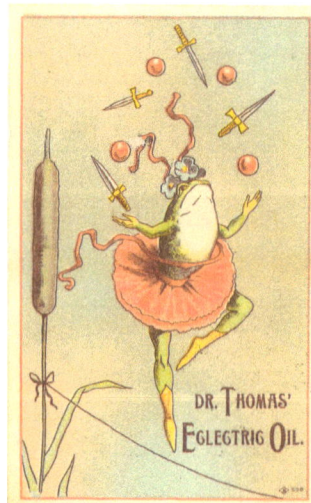

ARTIST: Unknown
Trade card
Late 19th C., U.S.A.
Chromo lithograph

ARTIST: Unknown
Trade card
Late 19th C., U.S.A.
Chromo lithograph

ARTIST: Unknown
Die cut scrap
Late 19th C.
Chromo lithograph

ARTIST: Unknown
Trade card
Late 19th C., U.S.A.
Chromo lithograph

ARTIST: Unknown
Trade cards
1880, U.S.A.
Chromo lithographs

ARTIST: Unknown
Trade card
Late 19th C., U.S.A.
Chromo lithograph

ARTIST: Unknown
Trade card
1894, U.S.A.
Chromo lithograph

ARTIST: Unknown
Postcard
Early 20th C., France
Chromo lithograph

GROUPED ANIMALS

"Of fowls after their kind, and of cattle of their kind, of every creeping thing of the earth after his kind, two of every sort…"

Genesis

ARTIST: Kathe
Olshausen-Schonberger
Book illustration
1903, Germany
Offset

ARTIST:
Charles H. Bennett
Book illustration
1857, England
Offset

ARTIST: Unknown
Book illustration
1893, U.S.A.
Chromo lithograph

ARTIST: Unknown
Book illustration
Late 19th C., England
Chromo lithograph

ARTIST: Unknown
Book illustration
Late 19th C., U.S.A.
Chromo lithograph

ARTIST: Unknown
Book illustration
Early 20th C., England
Offset

Dance with me

ARTIST: Unknown
Book illustration
Late 19th C., U.S.A.
Chromo lithograph

ARTIST: Unknown
Book illustration
Late 19th C., U.S.A.
Chromo lithograph

ARTIST: Unknown
Book illustration
Late 19th C., U.S.A.
Chromo lithograph

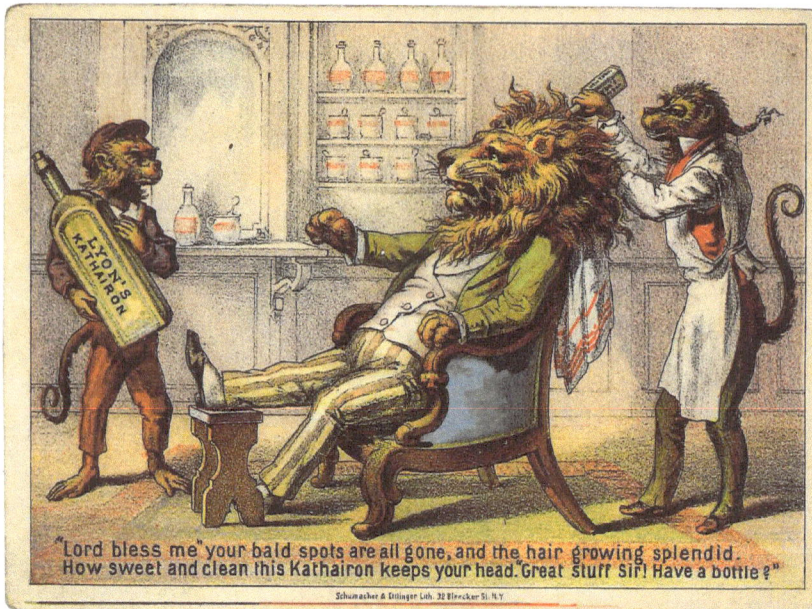

ARTIST: Unknown
Trade card
Late 19th C., U.S.A.
Chromo lithograph

"Lord bless me" your bald spots are all gone, and the hair growing splendid.
How sweet and clean this Kathairon keeps your head. Great stuff Sir! Have a bottle?"

Schumacher & Ettinger Lith. 32 Bleecker St. N.Y.

ARTIST: Kathe
Olshausen-Schonberger
Book illustration
1903, Germany
Offset

ARTIST: Unknown
Trade card
Early 20th C., Australia
Chromo lithograph

ARTIST: Unknown
Trade card
Late 19th C., U.S.A.
Chromo lithograph

ARTIST: Unknown
Trade card
Late 19th C., U.S.A.
Chromo lithograph

ARTIST: Unknown
Die cut scrap
Late 19th C.
Chromo lithograph

ARTIST: Unknown
Die cut scraps
Late 19th C.
Chromo lithographs

CHOCOLATES SELECTOS   EVARISTO JUNCOSA HIJO   DIPUTACIÓN, 114   BARCELONA

ARTIST: Unknown
Advertising booklet
Late 19th C., Spain
Chromo lithograph

ARTIST: Unknown
Die cut scrap
Late 19th C.
Chromo lithograph

Now why do you go in a series of hops
Asked the inquisitive Chanticleer,
I am hopping to the brewery sir
Where they need my hops for beer.

ARTIST: Unknown
Trade card
Late 19th C., U.S.A.
Chromo lithograph

ARTIST: Unknown
Trade card
1881, U.S.A.
Chromo lithograph

J. W. LeMAISTRE,
No. 48 North Eighth St., Philad'a
Embroideries, Laces, White Goods,
Lace Curtains, etc.,
Corsets and Gloves.

ARTIST: Unknown
Trade card
Late 19th C., U.S.A.
Chromo lithograph

ARTIST: Unknown
Trade card
Late 19th C., U.S.A.
Chromo lithograph

ARTIST: Unknown
Trade cards
Late 19th C., U.S.A.
Chromo lithographs

ARTIST: Unknown
Trade card
Late 19th C., U.S.A.
Chromo lithograph

ARTIST: Unknown
Trade card
Late 19th C., U.S.A.
Chromo lithograph

ARTIST: Unknown
Postcard
Early 20th C.,
Germany
Chromo lithograph

ARTIST: Unknown
Trade card
Late 19th C., U.S.A.
Chromo lithograph

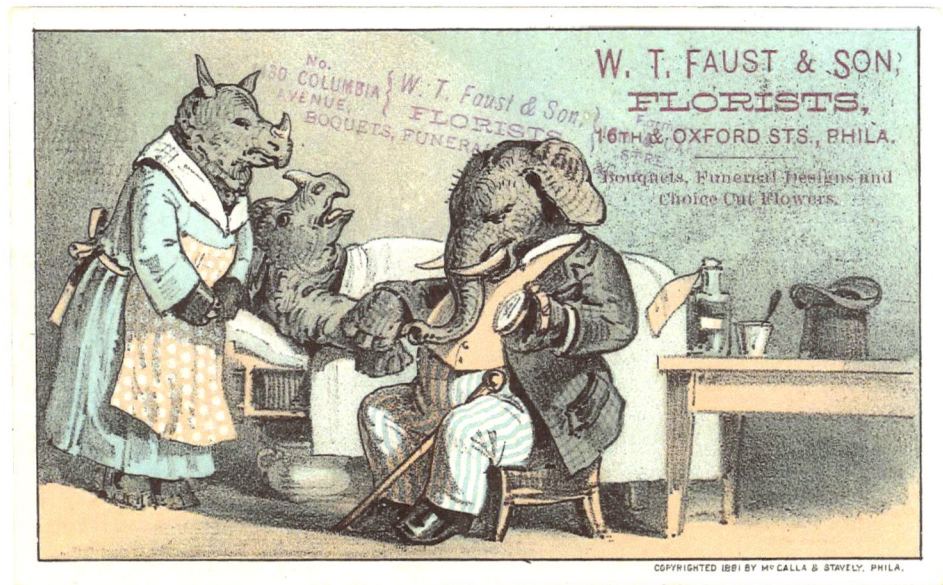

ARTIST: Unknown
Trade card
1881, U.S.A.
Chromo lithograph

"1er Avril"

Qu'on ait faim, c'est chose ordinaire!
Mais vous vous gavez, j'en réponds,
Et je vous le dis sans mystère,
Vous mangez comme des....cochons.

ARTIST: Unknown
Postcard
Early 20th C., France
Chromo lithograph

"1er Avril"

Le travail mène à la fortune.
L'art à la gloire où nous volons;
Mais, la chose est bien plus commune,
La cuite mène au violon !

ARTIST: Unknown
Postcard
Early 20th C., France
Chromo lithograph

206

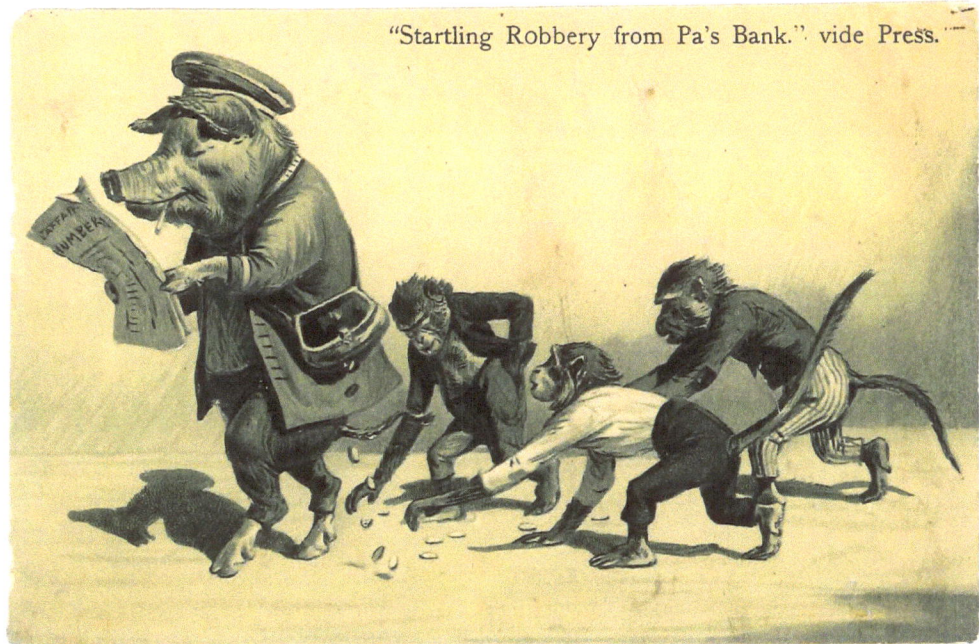

"Startling Robbery from Pa's Bank." vide Press.

ARTIST: Unknown
Postcard
Early 20th C., England
Lithograph

MR. LE BARON, MME. LA BARONNE ET LEUR FILS.

ARTIST: Unknown
Postcard
Early 20th C., France
Lithograph

Acknowledgments

First and foremost this book could not have existed without the skills, patience and love of my wife Joyce Zavarro. John Hammett's polymath abilities were of great help in writing the introduction. Professors Anthony Ranere and Wanda Corn were kind enough to review the early version of this book and offer their suggestions. Joel Forrester who kept at me to finish this formidable project. Ephemerists Bruce Shuer and Hannut Varise, for both supplying wonderful animal-people examples as well as their good wishes on the project. Frances March for copy-editing and feedback on introduction. The support of Sam and Isabel Gross, Greg and Jelena Twirbutt, Ron and Maria Blum, and Jay Wynshaw. And finally Tony Bly, whose belief in this project allowed me to press on to completion.

Bibliography

ALLEN, ALISTAIR, and HOVERSTADT, JOAN, *The History of Printed Scraps* (1983).

APPLEBAUM, STANLEY, *Bizarreries and Fantasies of Grandville* (1974).

AESOPS FABLES COMPLETE, (1900)?

FORBES, ROBERT and MITCHELL, TERENCE, *American Tobacco Cards: Price Guide and Checklist* (1999).

GUITON, MARGET, *Le Fontaine: Poet and Counterpoet* (1961).

HART, CYNTHIA, GROSSMAN, JOHN and DUNHILL, PRISCILLA, *A Victorian Scrapbook* (1989).

HOAGE, R.J. and WEISS, W.A. ed., *New Worlds, New Animals: From Menagerie to Zoological Park* (1996).

HOFER, MARGRET K., *The Games We Played: The Golden Age of Board and Table Games* (2003).

JAY, ROBERT, *The Trade Card in Nineteenth-Century America* (1987).

KADUCK, JOHN M., *Advertising Trade Cards* (1976).

KLAMKIN, MARIAN, *Picture Postcards* (1974).

LAMBOURNE, LIONEL, *Ernest Griset: Fantasies of a Victorian Illustrator* (1979).

LAST, JAY T., *The Color Explosion: nineteenth-century American lithography* (2005).

LEAR, LINDA, *Beatrix Potter: A Life in Nature* (2007).

MALLOY, ALEX G., *American Games: Comprehensive Collector's Guide* (2000).

MCCULLOCH, LOUIS W., *Paper Americana: A Collector's Guide* (1980).

MILLER, STEPHEN, *Walking New York: Reflections of American Writers from Walt Whitman to Teju Cole* (2015).

NEVINS, ALLAN, *A Century of Political Cartoons: Caricature in the United States from 1800 to 1900* (1944).

NICHOLSON, SUSAN BROWN, *The Encyclopedia of Antique Postcards* (1994).

PICARD, LIZA, *Victorian London: The Tale of a City* (2005).

RICKARDS, MAURICE, *Collecting Printed Ephemera* (1988).

RITVO, HARRIET, *The Animal Estate: The English and Other Creatures in the Victorian Age* (1987).

ROGER-MARX, CLAUDE, *Graphic Art of the 19th Century* (1962).

ROSTAND, EDMOND, Chantecler, (1910).

RYAN, DOROTHY B., *Picture Postcards in the United States 1893–1918* (1982).

SHIKES, RALPH E., *The Indignant Eye: The Artist as Social Critic* (1969).

SOREL, EDWARD, *Resemblances: Amazing Faces of Charles LeBrun* (1980).

TYTLER, GRAEME, *Physiognomy in the European Novel: Faces and Fortune* (1982).

TOMKINS, PTOLEMY, *The Monkey in Art* (1994).

WECHSLER, JUDITH, *A Human Comedy: Physiognomy and Caricature in the 19th Century Paris* (1982).

WEINSTEIN, AMY, *Once Upon a Time: Illustrations from Fairytales, Fables, Primers, Pop-Ups, and other Children's Books* (2005).

WHITTON, BLAIR, *Paper Toys of the World* (1986).

www.ingramcontent.com/pod-product-compliance
Lightning Source LLC
Chambersburg PA
CBHW060857270326
41935CB00003B/14